THE MIND TO
LEAD

COACHING FOR
CALM, CONFIDENT
POWER

Suzanne Kryder, Ph.D.

NeuroLeap Press

Requests for permission should be addressed to:

NeuroLeap Press
P.O. Box 11892
Washington, DC 20008
U.S.A.

Edited by Carolyn Flynn
Designed by Carolyn Flynn
Printed by CreateSpace
Illustrations by Mari Gayatri Stein

Library of Congress Cataloging-in-Publication Data
2011935907

Kryder, Suzanne, 1955-
        The mind to lead: Coaching for calm, confident power. Suzanne Kryder. 1st
edition.
        Includes bibliographical references and index.

ISBN 978-0-9838798-0-0
ISBN 978-0-9838798-1-7

DEDICATION

With love and appreciation for my family

TO THE READER

The Mind to Lead was written as a leadership development
resource, not as a medical guide or manual for treatment.

Its ideas and suggestions are designed
to help you develop tools and practices to make you
a more effective leader.
They're not intended to help you make a diagnosis about your
health or the health of anyone you know,
nor are they a substitute for any treatment that has been
prescribed by your doctor or health care provider.

If you suspect you have a medical problem, please seek
competent medical help. Before you use any methods from this
book, discuss that decision with your health care provider.

You, the reader, must take full responsibility for all
decisions about your health and how you use this book.

Therefore, the publisher disclaims any responsibility
for any adverse effects that result from your use
of the information in this book.

TABLE OF CONTENTS

WELCOME TO *THE MIND TO LEAD*

Karen's voice cracked nervously through the phone, "Hello."

I remembered how she approached me after a talk I recently gave at a conference. "I need your help. Really!"

I started our call by asking how she was doing. She admitted that it was a bit nerve-wracking to begin a professional coaching relationship on the phone with a total stranger who was thousands of miles away.

From the questionnaire Karen sent the day before, I knew she was 44 years old and an expert in her field. She'd spent most of her career since graduate school as a scientist, and more recently as a team lead who ran a small lab in the Research and Development division of a health care products company on the West Coast. When her longtime mentor and boss died unexpectedly three years ago, Karen reluctantly agreed to replace him as Director of R & D. Suddenly, she was overseeing a $4 million dollar budget with eight managers reporting to her. Other than a three-day management training program and some communications courses over the years, she had received no formal leadership development support.

I asked Karen where she wanted to begin our conversation.

"I don't know what I'm doing. I'm making a mess of things. They shouldn't have hired me to run this place. I should resign and go back to a technical position. That's when I was happiest."

A Bad Hair Day is nothing.

I wanted to save Karen from a Bad Mind Day.

My job is helping successful leaders like Karen notice that when they think poorly, they lead poorly. You can imagine how Karen's reactive thoughts impacted her inner confidence and her outer behavior. If she couldn't calm herself down, she wouldn't be able to authentically lead anyone on her team.

Like many leaders today, Karen had a simple though serious problem. Her mind was out of shape. She was distracted, alternating between regrets about the past and worries about the future. Regrets and worries are junk food for the mind. Karen's steady diet of negative thinking coupled with a lack of mental training created a sad state – an unfit, over-reactive, self-doubting mind.

Karen's mind needed a personal trainer – someone to help her regain mental flexibility, strength, and endurance for the long haul.

For more than 20 years, I've had the opportunity to train and coach thousands of leaders' minds to be less reactive and more adaptable and sturdy. In that time, I've seen how even the most successful leaders in a variety of sectors – nonprofit, education, government, and private – are still struggling to create lasting change in organizations. The source of their problems usually stems from how leaders manage themselves. So, before focusing on external communication skills, I first help leaders notice how they talk with and motivate themselves. The conversations they have with themselves are the most important conversations they have.

For example, many leaders, despite their outer success, are unkind and even degrading to themselves. I created the model and tools in this book to help leaders improve their own performance without forcing or shaming themselves. Other leaders have trouble staying calm or controlling emotional outbursts; my model helps them be confident and relaxed during the most challenging situations that in the past made their hearts race or tied their stomachs in knots. And, other leaders have trouble creating work-life balance; I help them not only say "No thank you" to activities and people that waste their time and energy but also make a commitment to renewal and silent reflection.

Ineffective communication is another very common challenge that even the most successful leaders have at times. For example, many leaders have trouble holding one or two resistant people accountable for commitments or are unable to repair a toxic communication culture of gossip, ridicule, and distrust. Other leaders are unable to resolve a pattern of ongoing interpersonal conflicts among their staff or colleagues.

I help leaders rectify all of these problems using one overarching skill: being mindful. Being mindful means stepping back and seeing a situation with objectivity – the part leaders play, the part others play, and realistic options for how everyone can calmly resolve the problem without being reactive.

By "being reactive," I mean responding without noticing what's happening or without consciously choosing appropriate steps to take. When we act more quickly than necessary, the result is frequently less than optimal. For example, when we're reactive, we're often angry or overly anxious, and our automatic response can worsen the problem, adding fuel to the flames or perpetuating a pattern that is harmful or unethical.

The mind is wired to notice and react quickly to threats. Slamming on the brakes to avoid an accident is an excellent use of your threat detection – or, "fight or flight" – mechanism. However, being overly aggressive and going into "fight" – like yelling at an employee who's late to work – or being overly passive and going into "flight" – like being silent when a colleague does something unethical – are often over-reactions to imagined threats. It may seem in the moment like you're doing the right thing; however, reactive behavior – responding without noticing – can worsen a problem. We don't always need to slam on the brakes or run and hide.

The antidote to being reactive is to notice what's happening. Simply observing can slow down your response and give you time to consider your options. Instead of overreacting, this book will teach you to notice what's happening in the present moment – even when it's extremely unpleasant or seems threatening – and to respond in a non-confrontational way to get better results. I call this mindful leadership style **Calm, Confident Power**.

I wrote this book for Karen and for all the leaders like her who are not only overwhelmed with increasingly complex responsibilities; they also lack the training to discipline their minds. The purpose of this book is to train your mind to lead.

And, the tool you'll use to buff up your mind *is* your mind.

Using your mind to get your mind in shape might sound confusing. You're probably wondering how the same mind that produces reactivity, worry, and judgments could also be a workout partner. While this might not make sense right now, your new mind motto is, "Use it to lose it." The Mind to Lead model will help you use your mind in new ways to lose the reactivity that increases your stress, lowers your confidence, and often leads to ineffective behavior.

THE BRAIN VERSUS THE MIND

In order to train your mind to lead, this book will explain enough about how the brain and mind work to help you understand and apply the tools. While scientists haven't completely agreed on the difference between the brain and mind, I want to distinguish how I'll use those terms in the book.

Because differentiating between the brain and mind is challenging, I'm taking a simple stance. The term "brain" will refer to the organ from which thought, emotion, and the control of body activities originates. The term "mind" will refer to the process that manages information flowing throughout the brain and body as well as between you and your external environment, which includes people, objects, and activities.

NEUROLEADERSHIP

This book will introduce you to a powerful, emerging field called neuroleadership. Neuroleadership is a term created in 2006 by David Rock, a thought leader in the global coaching profession, and Dr. Jeffrey Schwartz, a research professor of psychiatry at the UCLA School of Medicine. They explained neuroleadership as a combination of leadership development and information about the workings of the mind (Rock and Schwartz 2006).

My neuroleadership model, The Mind to Lead, develops a specific leadership style that I call Calm, Confident Power. Leaders who develop this style are able to smooth out the rollercoaster highs, lows, judgments, and fears of Bad Mind Days by strengthening a particular mind muscle. I call this muscle the **Reporter**.

THE REPORTER

Like a good leader, a good reporter is curious, unbiased, analytical, and focused. A good reporter separates her personal experience from what she's reporting on even if it's upsetting or personally threatening. As a result of noticing what's happening in the present moment, a reporter can stay calm in the midst of chaos. One famous example was Herbert Morrison, the Chicago radio correspondent who was taping a report about the Hindenburg in New Jersey in 1937. As it was landing, the large blimp exploded right before his eyes. Despite his shock, he composed himself enough to report on the rescue efforts and to interview survivors.

I'm not suggesting that leaders face the same level of trauma as Morrison or a war correspondent. However, being able to notice and describe what's happening in your experience with an unbiased attitude – even if you're having a strong reaction – can help you stay calm as well as think and act more clearly. The **Reporter** is another term for mindfulness – an awareness of the present moment.

The book includes case studies of my clients to help you understand the importance of mindfulness and the various levels of expertise that people have with it. I hope the stories encourage you to continually develop your mindfulness, because your **Reporter**'s ability level determines your success with The Mind to Lead model, with getting results, and with creating change in your organization.

For example, if you're new to mindfulness, you might feel like Jimmy Olson, cub reporter at *The Daily Planet*, who learned the ropes from Lois Lane and other experienced colleagues. That's okay. If you have an open mind and are willing to practice, you'll pick up the tools easily, and steadily rise to seasoned reporter. Many of my clients, on the other hand, come to coaching with a strong background in mindfulness. While their **Reporter**s aren't perfectly aware or fearless, many have made Pulitzer-Prize-winning shifts as a result of bringing mindfulness to their role as leaders.

The **Reporter**'s ability to *describe* what's happening in the present moment is called "labeling." Later in the book, you'll read about research on labeling. It's an effective way to calm the mind and body without repressing even the most negative experiences that you or others have.

It might sound counterintuitive to describe or label what's upsetting. Wouldn't it make more sense to ignore it, and move on? Unfortunately, ignoring an experience doesn't make it go away. If your boat is taking on water, ignoring your wet feet doesn't stop the water from rising. It's the same with work situations that bother you. So, labeling is the first tool I gave to Karen after she stated those upsetting thoughts about not knowing what to do.

SUZANNE: You're very aware, Karen. You just stated your negative thoughts clearly. How do you feel about them?

KAREN: I can't stand them.

SUZANNE: Let's talk about the difference between a thought and a feeling. 'I can't stand them' is a thought. What feelings or emotional states do you experience while you're having those unpleasant thoughts?

KAREN: I don't know what you mean.

SUZANNE: Feelings come in four general categories: mad, sad, glad, and afraid, with lots of flavors underneath each one.

KAREN: Oh, I get it. I feel mad that I don't know what I'm doing. I feel sad that I miss my old job. I'm worried and embarrassed that I'm not performing at a level that my team deserves.

SUZANNE: Great job describing your feelings, Karen. That skill is called labeling. How do you feel now?

KAREN: It's odd. I feel a little calmer. Like I can talk about my miserable experience with a little bit of distance. Is that normal?

SUZANNE: Yes, it's completely normal. Labeling is a skill I'd like to invite you to practice. As soon as your **Reporter** notices that you're getting upset, you can either write your thoughts and feelings down, or say them out loud. This practice will train your mind to notice and label your negative thoughts quickly.

KAREN: If all of this helps me stop thinking, I'll be happy!

SUZANNE: Let's manage your expectations. That's not going to happen. In fact, we don't want your mind to stop thinking. Hearts beat, and minds think. That's just what your mind does – all the time. Instead of stopping your thoughts, I want to help you *notice* that you're thinking, what you're thinking, and how your thoughts impact you. Then, I'll show you what to do with the negative thoughts in order to limit their harm.

KAREN: That sounds like a lot of work.

SUZANNE: You're a quick learner. I'll break it down into small steps that you'll pick up fast. Once you get the hang of it, you'll do the steps unconsciously. And, when you begin to see how much this process helps you stay calm, feel confident, and influence people, you'll be motivated to practice the tools regularly.

KAREN: Okay, I'll give it a try. I'm glad you think I can do this.

Based on my experience helping other leaders, I knew Karen could make significant changes to reduce her inner discomfort and improve her outer effectiveness. I didn't start out helping clients this way though. The Mind to Lead model evolved over 28 years of professional and personal growth.

The journey began about 1976 when I got hooked on yoga and relaxation techniques. By 1978, I had finished teaching two years of middle school in the mountains of northeast Georgia and decided to move to San Diego and work with adults. I got a job as the supervisor of a small title insurance office. I was 23 years old with no management experience or training, and I was the boss to two very high performers. Both were older and more experienced than me.

I was in way over my head.

After a few months of watching them ignore my misguided attempts to motivate them to higher performance, I gave up and became a passive supervisor – filling my days with inane tasks like opening the mail then sneaking away to the beach. I didn't realize at the time how this painful experience would later fuel my desire to help leaders – particularly new or untrained ones – suffer less.

A few years later, after I got my master's degree in exercise physiology, I started working in a fitness center where I also taught stress management classes. One day in class, when I asked how people were doing with the breathing exercises, a man replied, "I can do deep breathing all day long, but my boss is still a jerk."

That comment changed my life.

I realized that I could have a greater impact on people's health by shifting my focus from the *symptoms* of work stress to one of the *sources*: ineffective leadership. By that time, I was 30 and had chalked up two more management jobs. I had improved a bit. Though overall, I experienced firsthand that when a boss seems like a jerk, it might be less about her personality and more about what she was missing in leadership training and support.

So, in 1985, I started a doctoral program in health education and organizational behavior. As a result, I became a management trainer and, later in 1999, a leadership coach who specialized in helping people be firm and fair during their dreaded conversations. I got pretty good at it, and my clients had a lot of success at these conversations. Over time, though, people admitted that despite using the communication skills on the outside, they often still felt nervous and insecure on the inside.

That's when I realized that I had to integrate my personal and professional lives.

The week before I started my doctoral program, I went on a yoga retreat where we also learned mindfulness meditation. I got hooked on mindfulness and developed an almost-daily practice. Over the next 20 years, I spent more than a combined 12 months on silent mindfulness retreats that ranged from two days to six weeks.

I never planned to teach mindfulness to my clients, until I noticed that more and more people began asking, "What can I do during a conversation when my stomach's churning or my heart's racing with fear?" I realized I needed to share the tools that had helped me so much. That's when I created The Mind to Lead neuroleadership coaching model, which synthesizes mindfulness, communication skills, and other brain-based approaches for creating lasting change – without being passive or aggressive.

WHO THIS BOOK IS FOR

This book is for anyone who leads in any aspect of his or her life. You might own a small business, run a multinational corporation, or coach a youth soccer team. If you're passionate about motivating others – in a non-confrontational way – toward your vision of a better future, this book will help.

Some of the tools that I created are based on mindfulness meditation. However, it's not necessary to have a background in mindfulness to understand or use them. You can use the tools at work or in your personal life regardless of your religious or spiritual background or beliefs. And, if you have done mindfulness, you might find the tools helpful for deepening your practice in daily life.

HOW TO USE THIS BOOK

The book contains practical exercises for training your mind to lead. To make the most of it, I recommend that you keep a journal of your experiences with the exercises. Try each exercise two or three times before deciding if it's a fit for you or not and whether you want to continue using it on a regular basis. Write your own case studies of what worked and didn't work. To help you remember what's most important from the book, teach the model to people throughout your organization and in your personal life.

HOW THIS BOOK IS ORGANIZED

PART ONE, TRAINING THE MIND TO LEAD, describes why leaders suffer unnecessarily and how The Mind to Lead model reduces stress, strengthens mental focus, and allows you to create lasting change in a non-confrontational way. This section introduces just enough brain anatomy and physiology for you to understand how the model and tools work.

PART TWO, DEVELOPING THE THREE MINDSETS: CALM, CONFIDENT, AND POWERFUL LEADERSHIP, explains how to use three unique processes to cultivate the model's three mindsets. Each chapter includes (1) a link to a short assessment so that you can evaluate your strengths and gaps in the mindset, as well as (2) three simple steps and (3) several tools for cultivating the process that develops the mindset. For example, the three simple steps, **Notice - Breathe - Allow**, cultivate the Mindfulness process that over time develops a mindset of Calm.

PART THREE, MERGING THE MINDSETS FOR LEADERSHIP SUCCESS: MANAGING UP, DOWN, AND ACROSS, describes how nine of my clients applied The Mind to Lead model. To retain their anonymity and protect the confidentiality of our coaching, I changed identifying and personal information about them. In some cases, I also combined client situations to create composite characters while maintaining the veracity of their success with the tools. I hope their experiences inspire you.

To promote equity between singular personal pronouns, I alternate the use of "she/her" and "he/his" in every other chapter. This Preface begins with "she/her."

The book includes two types of boxes:

• **WORK OUT** boxes describe simple exercises to get your mind in shape. You can do most of the exercises in less than ten minutes. And, some of the tools in the exercises work in as little as five or ten seconds.

• **MIND TRICK** boxes summarize neuroscience research. They explain how aspects of your brain and mind can help your leadership success.

At the end of each chapter, there's a summary of key concepts like this:

CONCEPTS

• Neuroleadership is an emerging field that combines leadership development and information about the workings of the mind.

• Reactivity coupled with a lack of mental training can lead to an out of shape, self-doubting leadership style that doesn't get results.

• You can train your mind to develop a calm, confident leadership style.

• The **Reporter**, or mindfulness, is an unbiased awareness of the present moment.

• The **Reporter**'s ability to name what you're aware of is called labeling.

PART ONE

TRAINING THE MIND TO LEAD

Even though many leadership positions are inherently overwhelming and stress-ful, you can train your mind to stay calm and get lasting results. **Chapter 1** describes how a leader's mind is both the cause of, and the solution to, most suffering in the work place. **Chapter 2** introduces The Mind to Lead model as a way to develop the three mindsets that leaders most want: Calm, Confidence, and Power. **Chapter 3** takes you on an abbreviated tour of the brain and mind, so that you understand how the tools and exercises in this book work.

CHAPTER 1

LEADERSHIP SUFFERING IS OPTIONAL

THE PROBLEM: LEADERSHIP SUFFERING

At the beginning of our next coaching call, Karen was extremely discouraged.

KAREN: In the past six months, two of my managers have transferred to other divisions. Yesterday, a third manager said that he was leaving, too. Is this my fault? I'm afraid that more people, including key research staff, are going to jump ship.

SUZANNE: It's scary to think that you're one of the reasons that people might leave.

KAREN: On top of that, I'm overwhelmed with 100+ emails a day, personnel problems that my managers can't handle, a new lab opening in Germany next month, and added projects from my boss, Gary. Frankly, the only thing that I really want to do is publish research in my field, and I just can't find the time to write.

THE CAUSE OF LEADERSHIP SUFFERING: AN UNTRAINED MIND

SUZANNE: Karen, what I'm about to say might sound a bit crazy. No matter what's happening outside a leader – regardless of how challenging the people and events are externally – the root of suffering radiates from inside, from the mind. Our suffering is due, in large part, to the mind's tendency to resist what's happening.

KAREN: You mean I should accept all this chaos and not try to do anything about it?

SUZANNE: No, I don't mean that. Let's try something. Would you play a video in your mind of the past 24 hours? (I paused for five seconds while Karen closed her eyes and replayed her lousy day.) Can you notice where you resisted what was happening?

KAREN: Yes, of course I see that. I hated yesterday! I still feel tense and upset. I feel like I'm going to snap. Isn't that normal after getting bad news?

SUZANNE: I'm sorry it was such a hard day. I hear the fatigue in your voice. Yes, it's completely normal to react to what's happening. However, how much did getting tense help the situation?

KAREN: It didn't help at all. (Deep breath) It compounded my stress. I felt so much resistance to everything; it felt like I was even resisting myself.

SUZANNE: That's exactly what happens. An internal conflict. Your mind resists not just what's happening in events outside you, it also resists your reaction to the events. It's very painful. One model that might help you understand this internal conflict is called the Triune Brain. It explains the three layers of the brain and how each one has different job descriptions that sometimes compete with one another.

THE TRIUNE BRAIN

Scientists use a variety of models to describe the structures and functions of the brain. For example, the neocortex is divided into four lobes or general areas that relate to certain functions – such as the occipital lobe at the back of the brain relates to visual processing.

Another model is the Triune Brain that describes the three evolutionary layers of brain development over millions of years: the Reptilian Brain, Paleomammalian Brain, and Neomammalian Brain (MacLean 1990). In order to describe the Triune Brain to Karen, I took poetic license. I said that since her brain has three different layers, she could think of having three different "minds" or ways to process her experience. Sometimes, particularly when we're under a great deal of stress, the three minds have competing needs. This inner competition can compound our sense of suffering.

I asked Karen for a recent example when she did something embarrassing at work that she regretted.

> KAREN: That's easy. Last week, I was invited to present at the Senior Management meeting, and I made a fool of myself in front of the Vice President of Finance. Because I was nervous, I wanted to get to the conference room early. When I walked in, Larry was sitting in the chair I always use for my manager meetings. Without thinking, I blurted out, "Hey, that's my seat!" Of course, he looked shocked. It was so humiliating.

> SUZANNE: That does sound embarrassing. And, it's a good example. Let's use that experience to review the three brain layers and the processes that they regulate (Figure 1.1). Two cautions – the brain is much more complex than these three representational layers. And, some neuroscientists believe that the Triune Brain theory isn't as accurate as once thought. However, for our purposes, I feel it's a practical way to broadly introduce some of the structures in the brain and processes in the mind.

REPTILIAN BRAIN

I explained to Karen that the Reptilian Brain developed at the top of the spine about 300 million years ago. The Reptilian Brain, composed of the cerebellum and brain stem, controls self-regulation including breathing, heartbeat, daily rituals, and establishing and defending territory.

When Karen walked into the conference room, she was already nervous about her presentation. When she saw Larry, that immediate sense that it was "her" seat originated from the Reptilian Brain or **Territorial Mind.**

PALEOMAMMALIAN BRAIN

When mammals came into existence about 250 million years ago, the Paleomammalian Brain developed as a layer over the Reptilian Brain. The Paleomammalian Brain corresponds to the limbic system, which includes the amygdala, hippocampus, and hypothalamus. In general, this area of the brain processes emotions and memory.

To compare these two layers of the brain, the Reptilian Brain doesn't innovate or think outside the box; it does the same thing every day and doesn't know how to handle unique situations. The Paleomammalian Brain, on the other hand, developed so that life forms could adapt to and survive changes in the environment. Because the Paleomammalian Brain corresponds to structures that express emotion like anger and fear, it allows people to react to obstacles rather than accept them as they are.

Because Karen was nervous about the presentation before she walked into the room, her sympathetic nervous system was activated, and it didn't take much for her to feel threatened. Her upset feelings about Larry originated from processes in the Paleomammalian Brain, or the **Emotional Mind**. As Karen said, she blurted out, "Hey, that's my seat," without thinking.

FIGURE 1.1. THE TRIUNE BRAIN

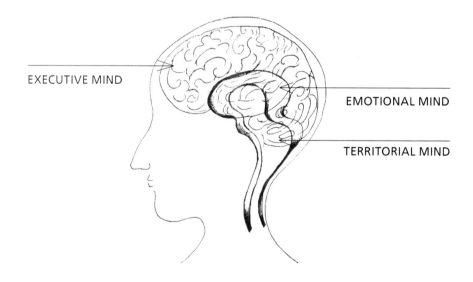

EXECUTIVE MIND

EMOTIONAL MIND

TERRITORIAL MIND

NEOMAMMALIAN BRAIN

The Reptilian and Paleomammalian brains co-existed for about 235 million years until another layer developed. The Neomammalian Brain evolved to perform high-level thinking like planning and conceptualizing. It corresponds to the neocortex of the brain. The neocortex is the quarter-inch thick, outermost layer of the brain. It's wrinkled, six layers deep, and is packed at birth with 100 billion brain cells, or neurons.

I asked Karen what happened after she overreacted to Larry.

> KAREN: My face turned red. Luckily, it just took me seconds to recover. I smiled at Larry, and calmly said, "I'm so glad that you're in it, and not me. That's where I sit during my manager meetings. I call it the Hot Seat, because sometimes they give me a hard time."
>
> SUZANNE: How did that go over?
>
> KAREN: Not great. He gave me a bit of a strange look, and said, "Oh, I see." Luckily, two other VPs walked into the room at that point, and we started talking with them.

Can you relate to Karen's story of overreacting to someone or something at work? (See the **MY LEADER REACTIVITY STORY Work Out Box**). It's relatively common, particularly when a leader is already feeling rushed or upset about something else. Even though the lower levels of her brain felt threatened, Karen's Neomammalian Brain stepped in quickly to analyze the situation, change the conversation, and attempt to make peace. I refer to these calming, stabilizing processes as the **Executive Mind**.

WORK OUT BOX
| MY LEADER REACTIVITY STORY

Sit quietly for a few minutes. Recall a time in the past when, as a leader, you overreacted to a situation or person. Write a brief description of the people involved and what each of you said and did. Reflect back to what was happening immediately prior to your overreacting. Were there extenuating circumstances that increased your stress and could have lead to your reactivity? What are the high-risk situations or people that tend to bring out your reactivity? What are the warning signals that you can *notice* next time you begin to get upset? Planning ahead, how would you like to handle a similar situation differently in the future?

KAREN: The three layers make sense. Is it possible for the Executive Mind to control the Emotional and Territorial Minds, so they don't get me in trouble?

SUZANNE: It's possible to train the Executive Mind to – I'd use the word influence, instead of control – the Emotional and Territorial responses. For example, research shows that mindfulness – which originates in the Executive Mind – can calm the natural reactivity in the Emotional Mind. However, I wouldn't expect miracles right away. Particularly in situations when you're already nervous or wound up – or even if you're extremely happy or excited – it's harder for the Executive Mind to prevent every emotional reaction. Using the Executive Mind to modulate the Emotional Mind is sort of like an adult calming a 4-year-old down. It's challenging enough on an average day. But, on his birthday, when there's cake, presents, and games, calm probably isn't going to happen.

KAREN: I get it. That's why I should have done a better job managing my anxiety about my presentation to senior management before I walked into the conference room.

SUZANNE: As you look back, what was happening that morning before your presentation?

KAREN: I was a wreck. I had stayed up until one in the morning finishing my slides and handouts. When I got to the office, there were two crises going on, a staff member's mother had died the day before, so we were trying to offer her support by phone. And, an internal customer was angry about a late deliverable. I had hoped to review my notes for the presentation and brainstorm questions they might ask. There just wasn't time.

SUZANNE: Play a video in your mind of yourself walking to the conference room. As you watch the video, label the thoughts and feelings out loud now that you were having then.

KAREN: I was thinking, "I'm going to blow this. I'm not prepared enough. The last time I presented, I ran over time." Let's see, what feelings was I having? Nervous, for sure. Angry that I didn't finish my slides earlier and get more sleep. Embarrassed that I probably wasn't going to do such a great job. There was also excitement about the data I would share, because it made my division look great.

SUZANNE: Good job labeling your thoughts and feelings, Karen. What was happening in your body?

KAREN: What do you mean? I was walking down the hall.

SUZANNE: How did your body feel inside? What physical sensations or experiences were you having?

KAREN: My stomach was in knots. My heart was pounding. My shoulders were pulled in toward my chest.

By replaying the experience in her mind, Karen was able to *notice* what happened physically, mentally, and emotionally. Next, I would ask her to *notice* her mind in even more detail. By the way, unless the word "mind" is preceded by one of the three layers – Territorial, Emotional, or Executive – I'm referring to the entire mind.

MIND TENDENCIES

In coaching leaders for many years, I've seen how the mind has two natural though unproductive tendencies that lead to suffering. Left to its own devices, the mind tends to:

1. Run a narrative about the past or future rather than relax in the present.
2. Respond to new experiences with old habits.

Let's look at each of these in more detail.

RUN A NARRATIVE ABOUT THE PAST OR FUTURE

Karen acknowledged that her thoughts probably compounded her anxiety. When

I asked her to *notice* the timeframe of her negative thoughts, she commented that her mind raced back and forth between remembering a poor presentation in the past and imagining that she would repeat her mistakes in the upcoming meeting. The mind is like a toggle switch. At any point in time, it's either aware of something that's happening in the present moment, or it's running a narrative – or story – about the past or future.

> KAREN: I can see how my thoughts were upsetting me in this situation. But, what's wrong with imagining the future? Olympic athletes use visualization all the time to mentally rehearse competitive events. If it works for them, why can't it work for me as a leader?
>
> SUZANNE: That's a valid point. I'm not against a conscious use of visualization to help you rehearse before an important event. I call it "playing a video." As the film's director, you get to imagine everyone in the scene saying and doing exactly what you want. Perhaps that could have helped you relax before your presentation. There's a difference, though, between intentionally rehearsing a successful performance and allowing your mind to run a nonstop scary movie about the past and future.
>
> KAREN: That's true. I don't want to do the horror movie anymore. When I'm anxious, I perform poorly.

It was an important insight on Karen's part. Since it was time for us to finish our call, I asked what action steps she wanted to take before our next conversation. She wanted to become more aware of the toggle switch in her mind and whether it was in "Now" or "Narrative." I thought that was an excellent idea, so we talked about ways to practice noticing her thoughts. (See **WHAT TIME IS IT IN MY MIND? Work Out Box**).

WORK OUT BOX

| WHAT TIME IS IT IN MY MIND?

Pick a routine task at work like putting paper in the copy machine or at home like having breakfast. While you do the task, *listen* to your thoughts as if you were listening to someone else talk. Don't try to edit or stop your thoughts. Simply *listen* for a minute or two.

What timeframe are your thoughts in? More than likely, they're not in the present or focused on the task you're doing. When you *notice* that your mind is running a narrative about something that either happened in the past or might happen in the future, gently say the word, "Narrative" in the back of your mind without saying it aloud. Noticing that your mind is in a narrative sometimes brings it back to the present moment. When your mind comes back to the present, *notice* the task you're doing. For example, if you're having breakfast, as you feel yourself move a spoonful of cereal into your mouth, label, "Now" gently in the back of your mind. Or, as you taste a sip of coffee or *notice* the smell of the fruit you're eating, label "Now."

If your mind continues to be distracted by a narrative about the past or future as you continue doing the task, that's normal. Try labeling "Narrative" or "Now" out loud. Hearing the labels may focus your mind on the task.

When you're finished, write in your journal what you noticed.

RESPONDING TO NEW EXPERIENCES WITH OLD HABITS

Perhaps you're beginning to notice that one source of suffering is the mind's lack of discipline. It misses the present when it's reliving the past or dreaming of the future.

Another performance gap in the mind is presuming that today will be just like yesterday. Imagine if a reporter who covered the Vietnam War was now a journalist in Iraq. And, instead of describing what was happening in Iraq, he read his old accounts of the fighting in Vietnam. You wouldn't get much new news.

Maybe you've noticed that instead of taking a fresh look at the people and projects it encounters each day, your mind tends to assume that work and life will be the same as before. For example, let's say you have an employee named Sam who has worked for you for nine years. As he walks into your office and before he even speaks, your mind opens the "Sam" file folder and silently repeats the contents: "Here he goes again. He talks too much. He doesn't get it. He never listens. He's got a lousy sense of humor." With strong beliefs like this, why even talk to Sam? Your mind not only believes it knows what he's going to say, it also knows you won't like it. Why does the mind react so quickly, habitually, and, for the most part, negatively?

THE SIX-FLOORED NEOCORTEX

Whenever you have a sensory experience, there's a great deal of activity in the six layers of the neocortex in the Executive Mind. Imagine that your neocortex is made up of elevator shafts, and each shaft has two elevators that carry information. One elevator full of information moves up from the bottom floor, and one elevator moves down from the top floor.

When you encounter a person – for example, your employee, Sam – new sensory information about him in the present moment comes into the body through the senses, moves up the spinal cord, into the brain stem and limbic system, enters the neocortex at the bottom floor and moves up the elevator shaft toward the processing floors at the top. That's called bottom-up processing.

Next, the neocortex sends old information that's "on file" about Sam from the past down from higher floors toward the lower input levels. Based on past experience, the upper floors "know" what Sam looks, sounds, and acts like. This is called top-down processing.

These waves of information meet in the middle around the third and fourth floors where the neocortex blends the two information streams. As a result of having a thick, pre-existing file on Sam, the old information on file tends to win out, and you're inclined to pay less attention to what he says and does today. You, also, lean toward responding to Sam in the same way you always have.

What's so bad about your memories of Sam trumping the new incoming sensory information? You're right; memory isn't all bad. You wouldn't want to wake up every morning and have to figure out who those people in your house are or how to drive a car.

Nevertheless, Dr. Dan Siegel says that when top-down processing wins, it not only limits the amount of new external information you process from people, places, and things. It also impairs your mind's ability to read your own cues. You lose touch with yourself and what you need to do in the present moment (Siegel 2007, 77). When top-down processing muffles your ability to take in novel data from yourself and others, you miss out on key information for making effective leadership decisions.

THE SOLUTION: TRAINING THE MIND TO LEAD

The good news is that you can train your mind to minimize its two tendencies – of running a narrative about the past or future and of responding habitually to new experience based on memory. Regardless of your age, your brain and mind are flexible. Scientists have discovered that the brain can reorganize itself by forming new neural connections (see **NEUROPLASTICITY Mind Trick Box**). These neuroplastic changes create structural modifications (the hardware looks different) that are accompanied by functional changes (software improvements). For example, many studies on mindfulness – or, being aware of the present moment – show that people experience functional improvements in emotional balance, immune function, and stress response. Let's look at mindfulness in more detail.

MIND TRICK BOX
| NEUROPLASTICITY:
YOU CAN TEACH AN OLD DOG NEW TRICKS

Neuroplasticity, also called brain plasticity or brain malleability, is the brain's ability to reorganize. Scientists have known for many years that neurons (nerve cells) in the brain reorganize in response to brain injury and disease. It's similar to when someone at work is out sick; your team reorganizes and forms new connections to cover his workload. The brain does the same thing. If one hemisphere is damaged, the other side of the brain may take over some of its functions. This happens because neurons communicate with each other via axons, their fiberlike extensions. Undamaged axons can grow new nerve endings to reconnect neurons whose links were injured or severed. This "axonal sprouting" forms new neural pathways to reinstitute a lost function. (Unfortunately, the technology to sprout new employees is not currently available.)

In order to reconnect, the neurons need to be stimulated by activity. For example, when my dad had a stroke, he underwent physical, speech, and occupational therapy in hopes of building new neural structures and regaining lost neural functions. Despite paralysis in his right leg immediately after the stroke, he eventually learned to walk again. Sadly, the damage to speech centers in his brain was too severe, and he never learned to talk again.

MINDFULNESS

Mindfulness refers to both the act of paying attention in the present moment as well as to a mind state that emerges as a result of paying attention. Mindfulness allows the mind to focus on the present moment so that a narrative about the past or future does not distract it. Mindfulness, which is also known as mindful awareness, is your **Reporter**. It lets you differentiate between the content of a sensory experience like the image of a tree versus the process of noticing that you are seeing.

In addition to focusing the mind in the present moment, Dan Siegel proposes that mindfulness inhibits top-down processing so that you are aware of more incoming new information via bottom-up processing and not so heavily influenced by the past (Siegel 2007, 106). Without mindfulness, your employee, Sam, looks and sounds the same as he has for the past nine years; and, your response to him is probably the same.

However, with mindfulness, you might notice details you weren't aware of before in his appearance, nonverbal cues, or behavior. Your new observations about Sam might lead you to listen more closely to his words, wonder about his motivation, or ask questions to draw out his ideas. When your behavior changes, Sam's behavior might change. When Sam changes, hopefully for the better, the team and the organization will improve, too.

This book can help you develop a new relationship with your mind. The exercises and tools will train your mind to notice when it's worrying or stuck in a narrative about the past or the future, resisting what's happening now, or mindlessly reacting out of habit. You'll learn to gently bring your mind back to the present, let go of struggles, and purposefully respond with greater effectiveness.

CONCEPTS

- The mind's two natural tendencies are to wander into a narrative about the past or future and to habitually respond based on past experiences.

- Neuroplasticity is the brain's ability to reorganize itself.

- Mindfulness studies have shown that subjects experience functional improvements in emotional balance, immune function, and stress response.

- Noticing that your mind is running a narrative can help bring your awareness back into the now or present moment.

CHAPTER 2

THE MIND TO LEAD MODEL: LEADERSHIP ATTUNEMENT CREATES CALM, CONFIDENT POWER

Karen was bubbling at the beginning of our next call.

> KAREN: Watching my thoughts is so cool! I'm having a blast. I thought leadership coaching would be about my direct reports. It's not. It's about me, isn't it?

> SUZANNE: Great insight, Karen. Coaching is about both. Have you got a piece of paper?

I had Karen draw the **Social Intelligence Grid** (Table 2.1), with rows labeled Self and Other and columns labeled Notice and Influence. The grid would help her understand attunement – or, getting a sense of what's going on for someone and then respectfully mirroring the person's experience back.

The Social Intelligence Grid is an application I developed by blending three concepts about the way we interact with others: multiple intelligences, social intelligence, and attunement. The first concept, multiple intelligences, was coined by Harvard psychologist Howard Gardner (1983). He identified seven kinds of intelligence, including 'intrapersonal' and 'interpersonal.' Dr. Gardner said that people with intrapersonal intelligence can understand and motivate themselves. People with interpersonal intelligence tend to empathize and communicate easily with others.

Author and former *The New York Times* science writer Daniel Goleman (*Social Intelligence: The New Science of Human Relationships*, 2007) added to the discussion on multiple intelligence when he wrote about the ideas of emotional and social intelligence. He described two broad categories of social intelligence: social awareness and social facility. He said that social intelligence is knowing what a person is feeling and then acting effectively based on that.

Dan Siegel, a UCLA neuropsychiatrist, explained attunement in *The Mindful Brain* (2007). He described how people use attunement to focus attention on the internal world of another. Attunement – whether with oneself or another – means getting a sense of what's going on for someone and then respectfully mirroring the person's experience back to her.

When attuning, you sense – through seeing, hearing, and intuition – what you think a person is experiencing physically, mentally, emotionally, and behaviorally. Then, you verbally and nonverbally communicate, 'I get it' back to her. She feels heard and understood, which builds positive feelings such as safety and trust. Over time, from interacting with you in this way, she may express more honest thoughts and feelings, because she trusts that she'll receive a respectful response. Leadership is about attuning both with yourself and each person you work with in order to develop open, productive work relationships.

TABLE 2.1 SOCIAL INTELLIGENCE GRID

	NOTICE	**INFLUENCE**
SELF Intrapersonal attunement	Notice self	Influence self
OTHER Interpersonal attunement	Notice other	Influence other

SUZANNE: When you practiced noticing the time frame of your thoughts, which cell were you in?

KAREN: Definitely noticing self. And, I think some self-influence, because I was trying to make myself pay attention to making a bowl of cereal. It was hilarious! I started out labeling "Now" quietly in my mind. But, I lost track and went back into "Narrative" thinking. Then, I remembered you said that labeling out loud could make it easier for my **Reporter** to stay focused. So, I started labeling out loud by saying, "Now" as I was pouring the milk, and "Now" as I was picking up my spoon. Then, my 10-year-old son, Josh, walked into the kitchen and freaked out. "Mom, what are you doing?!" I said, "My **Reporter** is labeling." He just rolled his eyes, and said, "Yeah, right." It was funny. I also tried labeling while eating the cereal. Oh, my gosh! The labeling helped. But, it's so hard to stay focused on what you're doing even if it's pleasant, like eating something good.

SUZANNE: You're having a lot of ah-has about noticing, Karen, and sounds like you're having fun doing it.

KAREN: Yes, it's great. I've tried using it a little bit at work, though I don't want to do labeling out loud. It's challenging to notice the time frame of my thoughts while I'm talking with someone. I get mixed up.

SUZANNE: That happens when you're new at labeling. I wouldn't recommend the Now/Narrative labels during a conversation. Instead, try using "Self" and "Other" to label how your noticing moves back and forth during a discussion. By the way, which cell were you in when you were labeling Now/Narrative during conversations?

KAREN: That was still self-awareness, because I was trying to notice what was going on inside me. Even though I got a bit confused with the labeling, it somehow made me more aware of listening to Janice and Bob. So, maybe it did improve my noticing of the other, too.

SUZANNE: You're talking about social intelligence. It's similar to how a tennis player monitors both herself and her opponent. A mindful leader does that, too, by oscillating awareness between her own and the other person's experience. In conversations, I recommend that leaders focus more than half of their awareness on noticing the other person. Also, *notice* the boundary between yourself and the other. By boundary, I mean the psychological borderline where you stop and the other person begins. Without clear boundaries, people sometimes get confused about who is feeling or thinking what.

KAREN: I know what you mean. Bob was upset that Janice's team was holding up a report. At one point, Janice looked at Bob and said, "You're accusing my team of being incompetent." I was shocked, though I let Bob respond. He stayed very calm, and said, "I've never said or thought that, Janice. What have I done that makes you think that?" It turned out to be a great conversation, because they resolved the tension as well as set a new deadline for the report.

SUZANNE: Bob showed social intelligence by staying calm despite Janice's accusation. Then, he skillfully influenced her behavior by asking an open-ended question.

KAREN: Yes, his question completely diffused the situation. She admitted that he hadn't done anything mean, and that she was assuming the worst. It was a perfect opportunity for me to talk about future thinking and how the mind tends to go negative when we're already stressed out. They both nodded their heads. It was awesome, Suzanne.

SUZANNE: You're stepping outside your comfort zone and trying lots of new behaviors, Karen. Congratulations!

KAREN: Thanks. It's been a little scary. Though, I've felt so much better in the last week. Not so overwhelmed. And, when I do get upset at work, I just take a moment to *notice* what I'm thinking about. Doing that helps, because I see that I'm usually worrying about the past or future.

SUZANNE: Good work. Let's go back to what you said about labeling as self-influence. Technically, labeling is noticing rather than influencing. As you play a video of yourself labeling your breakfast, can you see that your **Reporter** was noticing events that were happening Now rather than dictating what would happen next?

KAREN: Yes, I see that now. I was noticing the present moment, rather than influencing my behavior. What's a tool for influencing the self? I need that! Badly!

SUZANNE: Conversation. The most important conversations are the ones you have with yourself. Most leadership development books and courses emphasize the 'Influence Other' cell. They teach external communication skills such as delegation, motivation, and performance management. Those are important skills. However, if a leader only talks with others and doesn't talk honestly with herself, she's missing a foundational piece – intrapersonal attunement – knowing both what motivates and immobilizes her.

KAREN: Are you saying that I can't lead others until I can lead myself?

SUZANNE: Keep going with that thought.

KAREN: If I can't shape my own behavior, how can I expect to influence someone else? That's why I was so excited to learn about my thinking, share my insights with Janice and Bob, and see that it helped them. And, see that they have the same kinds of thoughts as I do. The more I learn to listen to, empathize with, motivate, and reward myself, the better I'll be at those skills with others.

SUZANNE: That's leadership, Karen. (She was doing all the work for me!) That's why I created The Mind to Lead model. It's a social intelligence framework for helping leaders notice and influence

themselves, first, so that they can use the same skills with others.
You did an outstanding job with labeling. I'd like to invite you to
bring even more awareness to your inner dialogue.

After discussing attunement, I gave Karen instructions for listening to her inner
dialogue and emphasized that she write it as one thought per line, rather than as a con-
tinuous monologue (see **LISTENING TO YOUR INNER DIALOGUE Work Out Box**).

MIND TRICK BOX
| ATTACHMENT THEORY

Learning to attune with self and others begins at birth when a mother or father
uses verbal and nonverbal communication to mirror an infant's emotions. For
example, when a baby cries, the parent might say, "Oh, you sound sad. I'm
sorry it hurts." This process of a parent attuning with the baby creates a basis
for emotional attachment.

Attachment theory was first developed by John Bowlby. It explains how
individuals learn about emotions and how to form emotional bonds with each
other. Since an infant isn't able to regulate her own emotions, she needs the
help of her caregiver. Research shows that how an infant learns to regulate her
emotions depends heavily on how her caregiver regulates his/her own emotions.

Attachment theory also describes the impact of those early bonds on a
person's later adult relationships. The brain uses childhood experiences to form
and archive mental models of self, others, and relationships. If as an infant, a
person experienced secure relationships with adult caregivers, she will tend to
have secure relationships as an adult and believe that other people are there for
her (Crawley and Grant 2005, 83).

On the other hand, insecure attachment experiences as an infant can lead
to unconscious beliefs as an adult that people aren't there for you and will
ignore or hurt you (Crawley and Grant 2005, 83). Therapy can provide some
of the missing attachment experiences so that the individual can learn affect
regulation – how to express and control one's emotions – and empathy.

Attachment theory has important implications for leaders. The sad news is
that some people didn't get a secure attachment base or enough relationship
glue from their parents to help them feel safe or do right as adults. As a result,
they might have a harder time interacting at work particularly with authority
figures. The good news is, thanks to neuroplasticity, even unhappy adults can
learn attunement skills, develop more secure attachment, and possibly change
the structure and function of their brains.

WORK OUT BOX
| LISTENING TO YOUR INNER DIALOGUE

The goal of this exercise is to be able to hear and write your thoughts in concise sentences. It is a foundational skill that you will use for other Work Outs in the book. Follow these steps to connect with your inner conversation.

1. Sit in a quiet room by yourself. To avoid interruption, close the door and turn off your phone and computer speakers.

2. Put a piece of paper and a pen or pencil in front of you.

3. Let your mind free associate. Let it roam wherever it wants to, and write down each thought you have in a short, simple sentence. It doesn't matter what the sentences are about; they might be about work, your personal life, or how you feel about this exercise. Try not to edit your thoughts. Write down everything that comes to your mind even if it sounds negative or irrelevant.

4. If you begin to repeat a thought or have a mental block, for example, "I can't think of anything else" or "This isn't getting me anywhere," put your pen down for a few minutes, sit in silence, and *listen* to your thoughts. If your mind is empty, that's fine. Enjoy the lack of thoughts even if it's just for a few seconds. Eventually, your mind will generate thoughts again.

5. If you like, you can jump-start your inner dialogue by reflecting on an issue in your work or life right now. *Listen* to your thoughts about that issue. Write them down in short sentences.

6. After five to ten minutes of listening to and writing your thoughts, sit in silence for one minute and *notice* how you feel. Write in your journal what you noticed during this exercise.

THE MIND TO LEAD MODEL

Over the past twenty years, I've trained and coached thousands of leaders. During that time, I listened for patterns in what they talked about, what was important to them, and how they described their hopes and fears. In analyzing my observations, I concluded that what leaders want most are strong inner qualities that they can rely on in any challenging situation. I synthesized the qualities they want into three mindsets:

1. Calm Leader
2. Confident Leader
3. Powerful Leader

First, leaders want to know that no matter what happens, they will be able to think and act calmly. They want to role-model composure to others and show people a way through the storm. When they were unable to do this, to stay calm under pressure, many of my clients deeply regretted instances of emotional reactivity – of yelling at or demeaning someone, or of experiencing severe anxiety during a challenging conversation with an employee, boss, or client.

In addition to staying calm, leaders want to feel confident on the inside and show it on the outside despite their constantly changing responsibilities and organizations. However, many leaders lack self-assurance as evidenced by the growth in sleep disorders and other stress-related health issues. Being unsure about the people and projects that you manage is painful enough; being uncertain about yourself and your ability to lead is doubly agonizing.

Staying calm and confident are the inner foundations for expressing power appropriately. Some people react negatively to the word "power," because it sounds like control or dominance to them. I don't think of power that way. I believe that a calm, confident leader uses her authority responsibly to influence others' behavior and reach organizational goals. Leaders often tell me that their greatest fulfillment at work comes from influencing others. Their influence ranges the gamut from encouraging an employee to finish graduate school to persuading a client to sign a multimillion-dollar contract.

FIGURE 2.1 LEADERSHIP ATTUNEMENT MODEL

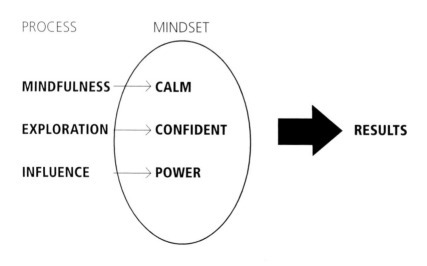

HOW DO YOU GET THERE?

After identifying the three mindsets, I worked backwards to create a brain-based coaching model that would help leaders achieve their desired outcomes. As I explained to Karen, social intelligence provided the theoretical framework I used to create The Mind to Lead attunement model; attunement is a skill set that socially intelligent people develop.

Each of the three leadership mindsets – Calm, Confident, and Powerful – is a result of practicing a particular attunement process. Calm leadership develops from the Mindfulness process, Confident leadership from the Exploration process, and Powerful leadership from the Influence process (Figure 2.1).

This book describes in detail how to cultivate each process for improved intrapersonal and interpersonal attunement. Improved attunement leads both to better work relationships and organizational results. Let's look at how each attunement process cultivates one of the mindsets.

THE *MINDFULNESS* PROCESS HELPS YOU STAY CALM

Mindfulness is paying attention nonjudgmentally to what's happening right now in your experience. Your experience comprises what I call the four realms: physical, mental, emotional, and behavioral. For example, right now, you can pay attention to the physical realm of experience by noticing the sensations of holding a book or to the mental realm of experience by noticing your thoughts about this book.

How does mindfulness lead to a sense of calm or nonreactivity? Scientists think that mindfulness induces nonreactivity by altering the connection between the prefrontal cortex in the Neomammalian Brain and the limbic system in the Paleomammalian Brain. The limbic system includes a pair of almond-shaped structures called amygdalae; there's an amygdala deep in each hemisphere of your brain, not on the surface of the cortex as it appears in this drawing (**Figure 2.2**). They're involved in the fear response known as "fight or flight," which, when activated, includes rapid heartbeat, increased respiration, and stress-hormone release. When the amygdala senses a threat, it's like stepping on the accelerator of your nervous system.

FIGURE 2.2 AMYGDALA AND PREFRONTAL CORTEX

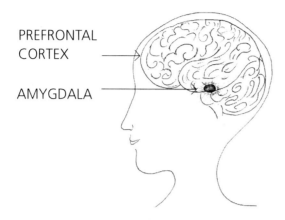

PREFRONTAL CORTEX

AMYGDALA

However, bringing mindfulness to your experience activates the prefrontal cortex – the area in the neocortex behind your forehead – which calms the amygdala's response; it's similar to putting on the brakes. In **Chapter 4**, you'll learn a variety of tools for using mindfulness to stay calm and focused in your work and personal life.

THE *EXPLORATION* PROCESS HELPS YOU BE CONFIDENT

Confidence is the belief or trust in a person's ability to act in a reliable way. Sometimes, leaders don't believe in their decisions, in themselves, or in other people. This lack of confidence is evidenced by their apprehensions ("I'm not sure if I should do this"), self-judgments ("I'm too tunnel vision; I'm not considering enough options"), and other-judgments ("She's arrogant. She's going to get it wrong").

In **Chapter 5**, you'll learn how to identify and explore these kinds of stressful thoughts about yourself and others using a methodology created by Byron Katie called **The Work**© (Byron Katie 2003, 2006, 2008). The Work© is a series of questions that I, along with many of my coaching clients, have found invaluable for noticing and neutralizing stressful thoughts, building confidence, and getting results.

While The Work © isn't a psychological therapy, it does have some similarities to cognitive behavioral therapy (CBT). CBT is based on the premise that our thoughts, rather than external things like people or situations, cause our feelings and behaviors. CBT presumes that irrational thinking patterns – called automatic thoughts – trigger ineffective behavior. CBT works to change the distorted thoughts by investigating their rationality and validity. Though it's not a therapy like CBT, The Work© is similar in that it explores the validity of stressful thoughts.

MIND TRICK BOX

| A NEW DRUG: THINKING STRAIGHT

Neuroscientist Helen Mayberg isn't very popular with the pharmaceutical industry. In 2002, she discovered that inert pills (placebos) worked the same on the brains of depressed people as the antidepressant, Paxil, did. With either pill, activity in the frontal cortex increased; activity in the limbic or emotion area, decreased. She wondered if cognitive behavioral therapy (CBT), or teaching people to view their stressful thoughts differently, would have the same impact on brains as Paxil and placebos did.

Along with colleagues at the University of Toronto, Mayberg took positron emission tomography (PET) brain images of depressed adults before and after two different treatments (Goldapple 2004, 35). Some of the adults received the antidepressant Paxil, while others got multiple sessions of CBT. In the CBT training sessions, subjects learned to break the habit of perceiving minor setbacks as tragedies. For example, a leader might realize that a direct report's blank face in a meeting doesn't mean that she hates you; she might simply be sleep-deprived from staying up late the night before to finish a project.

Results showed that depression lifted in all of the patients, regardless of whether their brains got a powerful drug or a different way of thinking. Scientists expected the brain scans at the end of this study would show similar results to the placebo study. But instead of increasing the frontal cortex/higher thought area like the antidepressant and placebo did, the CBT decreased activity in the frontal cortex. And, instead of lowering activity in the limbic/emotion center of the brain like the antidepressant did, the CBT raised activity in the limbic system (Goldapple 2004, 38).

Dr. Mayberg's team concluded that while both treatments – Paxil and CBT – brought relief from depression, CBT moves in the brain in a different direction than Paxil. CBT has been considered a top-down approach, because it focuses on decreasing negative thinking functions in the neocortex. This allows normal mood states to increase from below in the limbic area. Drug therapy, on the other hand, is considered a bottom-up approach because it alters the chemistry in the limbic area to decrease negative emotional response, and that results in an increase in productive thinking in the cortex upstairs.

THE *INFLUENCE* PROCESS HELPS YOU USE POWER

The first two processes in The Mind to Lead model – Mindfulness and Exploration – happen internally. Mindfulness uses a relaxed, neutral **Reporter** to collect information from all four realms of your experience. The next process, Exploration, occurs in the mental realm. Exploration lets you investigate any stressful thoughts to determine if they are accurate or not, and whether they are building or undermining your confidence. After you complete these two internal processes, the Influence process allows you to externally communicate a calm, confident message to others.

In **Chapter 6**, you'll learn to communicate succinct messages that influence others to act. You'll also learn to reduce resistance to your message, in order to efficiently delegate tasks and hold people accountable for their assignments. Then, the nine case studies in **Chapters 7 – 9** share examples of how my clients used the three processes successfully with bosses, employees, and colleagues.

CONCEPTS

- Intrapersonal attunement uses your **Reporter** to listen and reflect back your own experience in the four realms: physical, mental, emotional, and behavioral.

- Interpersonal attunement uses your **Reporter** to oscillate awareness between your own and another person's experience. In conversations, focus primarily on the other person's experience. Also, notice your own experience as well as the boundary between yourself and the other person.

- Leaders can cultivate the three mindsets they most want – Calm, Confidence, and Power – by practicing three attunement processes: Mindfulness, Exploration, and Influence.

- The Mindfulness Process uses the prefrontal cortex to relax and focus the mind on the present moment.

- The Exploration Process uses questions to investigate the validity of stressful thoughts. Recognizing that the thoughts are untrue builds confidence and motivates clear action.

- The Influence Process helps you communicate concise messages and, when needed, quickly reduce resistance to your stated expectation.

CHAPTER 3

HOW YOUR BRAIN & MIND WORK

When she called for our next coaching conversation, Karen's voiced was hushed and concerned.

KAREN: Suzanne, watching my thoughts is creepy.

SUZANNE: It's scary to try something new, Karen. What's been happening?

KAREN: I wrote down my thoughts like you suggested. They're all negative. They're so judgmental and demanding. I'm THE most critical person on the planet!

SUZANNE: I heard a slight giggle in there, Karen.

KAREN: Well, my thoughts are so petty that it's funny. I guess. Isn't it?

SUZANNE: A sense of humor can be helpful when we're watching our thoughts. What's the worst thing you wrote?

KAREN: The worst one was about one of my managers. I've talked about Janice with you before. I wrote, "Janice is a dull, lifeless slob." I'm so embarrassed I think that about her. She does a good enough job. Why do I care about her personality or clothes?

SUZANNE: That's just what minds do, Karen. Did you have a particularly negative experience with Janice in the past?

KAREN: Yes, it was terrible. It was five years ago. We were on a panel presentation together at a conference. She accused me in front of the whole audience of, not falsifying data, but of exaggerating my findings. I defended myself calmly, and several people spoke up to disagree with her. However, the damage had already been done. Her accusation was the buzz for the rest of the conference. I was livid. And, I felt completely betrayed, because the week before the conference, I had asked her to give me feedback on my paper. She said it was fine.

SUZANNE: Karen, that's such a difficult situation with so many different unpleasant feelings. I can see how embarrassing it would be to have someone falsely accuse you in public. Plus, you were angry. And, she is your colleague, who you thought you could trust. That's scary as well as maddening.

KAREN: It was a big mess. On the flight home, I tried to tell Janice how angry I was. She apologized, though I didn't believe that she meant it. Then, two years later when Richard died unexpectedly, Janice got really mad at me. She felt that I was handed the promotion instead of her application being considered. I have to hand it to her though. Once I became her boss, she never gave me any problems again. She's never questioned any of my decisions or resisted assignments. I'm not angry about the conference any longer; I just don't trust her like I used to. Is that why I'm more judgmental of her than other people?

SUZANNE: There's no simple answer, Karen. Your relationship with Janice is complex. There's a lot of history, changing roles, and power dynamics that your mind is sorting out. If you'd like to talk about some possible approaches to rebuilding trust with her, I'd be happy to do that on this call or in the future. First, though, I'd like to address some of your comments and questions about negative thoughts.

A body of research theorizes that the brain has a "negativity bias." For example, Marcus Raichle (2001) and his colleagues say the brain has a "default mode" of tracking threats when a person is at rest. This constant tracking is how early humans survived. People who were vigilant and always on the lookout for danger were the ones who stayed alive and had more offspring. As a result of evolution, people today have a relatively overdeveloped sensitivity for threats and negativity. So, it's normal that during the exercise while Karen sat quietly, a lot of negative thoughts popped up in her mind. It happens to all of my clients. We all have negative thoughts even about people we like and love. I asked Karen if she *noticed* that.

> KAREN: Yes, I did. During the exercise, a memory of my husband taking me out for a wonderful birthday dinner popped into my mind. The first thought I wrote was, "Dinner was fun." The next thought was, "He really needs a haircut." That's silly. It's so unimportant compared to what an amazing person he is. Luckily, I keep those trivialities to myself.

> SUZANNE: I'm glad you could see that the mind judges most everyone. It makes sense that you would have stronger negative judgments about Janice. Again, as a result of evolution, the people who could not only detect danger signals most quickly and accurately, but could also store, recall, and act on that information, were the ones who survived. Even though Janice is no longer a threat, your brain is slow to forgive and forget. Psychological research shows that it takes five positive exchanges with a person to outweigh one negative interaction (Gottman 1995). So, your brain is keeping score with Janice.

I can't say for sure why Karen was more judgmental about Janice than anyone else on her team; other members have also let her down at some point over the years. However, I could theorize that it had to do with the incident at the conference. There's a field of research called trauma memory that studies how people store and access memories of traumatic experiences. Because the amygdala – the threat detection center – is located next to the hippocampus – a memory storehouse – scientists believe that when we experience a very strong negative emotion in the amygdala, the associated memories get priority storage in the hippocampus.

For example, I remember very clearly what happened the day that President Kennedy was shot. Even though I was only seven years old, I can still see the nun in my elementary school announcing that we were being sent home. And, I remember when I got home, my mom smoking cigarettes while she nervously watched the news reports on television. Since then, I've lived thousands and thousands of days that I have no memory of. Because it was such a chilling experience, my hippocampus – even five decades later – gives me easy access to those memories.

KAREN: So, the conference is a traumatic memory?

SUZANNE: I'm not a therapist. I don't know if it qualifies as a trauma. Do you have a strong memory of the event?

KAREN: Yes, painfully so. When I think about it, I can remember my heart pounding and my hands sweating in my lap. I see myself looking out into an audience of mostly unfriendly faces while Janice trashes me. It's not as strong a memory now, though it was horrible at the time.

SUZANNE: It sounds incredibly upsetting. Like the rug was pulled out from under you. Can you feel that you're not there right now?

KAREN: Absolutely. I'm fine. I know that I'm safe right now, sitting in my office and talking with you on the phone. Janice doesn't scare me anymore. I just wouldn't trust her with any secrets.

SUZANNE: That sounds reasonable. It also sounds like you're understanding how the mind holds onto negative information in order to help you protect yourself. Your judgments of Janice might seem a bit strong though not outside the ordinary, given your experience with her. If you'd like to, at some point, we can talk about how to investigate how they impact your interactions with her. And, if you're interested in learning more about how to manage the brain's negativity bias, I highly recommend Rick Hanson's book, *Buddha's Brain: The Practical Neuroscience of Happiness, Love, and Wisdom* (2009). You can also listen to radio interviews I did with Dr. Hanson and Dr. Dan Goleman, by going to goodradioshows.org. Click on

Peace Talk Episodes in 2009.

KAREN (laughing): I guess this means I'm not THE most critical person on the planet.

SUZANNE: No, you're simply one of billions. Would you like to try another mind exercise? This one might help calm the judging a bit.

KAREN: I'm very interested in that! I'm determined to get this brain of mine in shape.

SUZANNE: You're becoming a mental fitness fanatic. I'd like to invite you to try some silent mindfulness practice. Before that, though, let's take a quick tour of the brain, so that you know a bit about the basic structures and functions involved in mindfulness.

THE BRAIN

An adult brain weighs approximately three pounds and is about the size of a grapefruit. The upper portion of the skull, or cranium protects the brain. Inside the cranium, a liquid bath protects and cushions the brain.

There are various maps of the brain. In addition to the Triune Brain model that I described in **Chapter 2**, the brain is divided into three anatomical sections – the cerebrum, cerebellum, and brain stem.

FIGURE 3.1 SECTIONS OF THE BRAIN

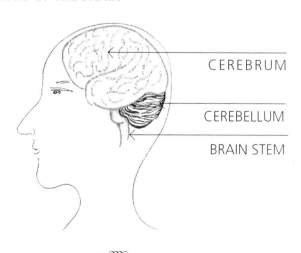

CEREBRUM

CEREBELLUM

BRAIN STEM

The cerebrum is the thinking brain where functions like language, memory, and sensations occur; it makes up about 9/10 of the whole brain. The cerebrum is divided into two halves called the right and left cerebral hemispheres that are connected by a thick band of nerves. The left hemisphere controls the right side of the body and the "L's" – language, logic, linearity, and literal thinking. The right hemisphere controls the left side of the body as well as artistic and emotional expression, insight, spatial relations, and autobiographical memory.

The cerebrum includes the cerebral cortex, which is divided into four sections, called lobes. Each lobe houses important functions:

• **PARIETAL**: sense of touch, pressure, and pain
• **OCCIPITAL**: sense of sight
• **TEMPORAL**: senses of smell and sound
• **FRONTAL**: conscious thought, parts of speech and movement, emotions, and the all-important prefrontal cortex

The prefrontal cortex (PFC) is behind your forehead at the front of the frontal lobe. It plays an important role in complex thinking, emotions, behavior, personality, and mindfulness. The PFC is the home of the executive function, which orchestrates thoughts and actions based on internal goals or intentions. Executive function is also responsible for:

• Predicting the future consequences of current behavior.
• Differentiating between conflicting thoughts ("I should stay in bed a little longer" versus "I better get up right now").
• Delaying immediate gratification in order to reach a better long-term outcome or reward.

The PFC doesn't reach full maturity until about age 25. If you manage young people, keep in mind that they are still learning how to use their executive function.

Deep inside the cerebrum is the limbic system, or Paleomammalian Brain. This system contains the thalamus, hypothalamus, hippocampus, and all-important amygdala. Each structure plays a unique role:

• The **thalami** are two bullet-shaped structures of grey matter that lie side by side, roughly in the middle of your brain. The thalamus is the receptionist or relay station between your brain, spinal cord, and body. Messages come up from the body through the spinal cord to the thalamus, which routes them to the appropriate area in the cerebrum. Outgoing signals are sent out through the thalamus to the appropriate part of the body.

• Right underneath the thalamus is the **hypothalamus** that regulates body temperature and responses like hunger, thirst, and fatigue. It's the part of your brain that signals the language center to communicate, "Coffee!"

• The **hippocampus** plays major roles in memory and spatial navigation.

• The **amygdalae** are the almond-shaped structures in the temporal lobes of the brain. Their primary role is the processing and memory of emotional reactions such as rage, sexual feelings, and the fear response known as "fight or flight." The reactivity of the amygdala can be calmed by the PFC.

The cerebellum and brain stem make up the Reptilian Brain. The cerebellum looks like a miniature brain. It's located underneath the cerebrum and has two hemispheres. It controls muscle movement, posture, and coordination. The brain stem lies below the limbic system. It regulates automatic body functions like heartbeat and respiration.

Now that you have a map of key structures in the brain, let's look at some of the functions they control.

MIND TRICK BOX
| STUDYING THE BRAIN

Scientists have invented a variety of sophisticated technologies for measuring brain health and activity. When you read about research in this book or elsewhere, this list will help you understand how scientists conducted the studies.

• **Electroencephalogram** (EEG): uses electrodes attached to the scalp to measure electrical impulses and brain waves such as alpha, beta, and gamma.

• **Computed Axial Tomography** (CAT): uses X rays to see many layers of brain tissue taken from different directions.

• **Magnetic Resonance Imaging** (MRI): a larger scanner uses magnetic fields and radio waves around a subject's head to produce high quality two- or three-dimensional images of brain structures.

• **Functional Magnetic Resonance Imaging** (fMRI): uses the changing blood flow in the brain to measure it at work. While MRI shows brain structures, fMRI shows which regions are more active while a subject does something such as viewing images, hearing sounds, or touching stimuli.

• **Positron Emission Tomography** (PET): uses emissions from radioactive chemicals injected into the blood stream to measure activity in various regions of the brain. Because the radioactivity loses its glow rapidly, PET is used to study short-term tasks.

"DANGER, WILL ROBINSON"

Wouldn't it be great if, like the young Will Robinson on "Lost in Space" (1965-1966), you had a robot to warn you of impending danger? Actually, you do. Your brain is sensitive – oftentimes super sensitive – to what's called "error detection." According to your brain, an error is anything that it didn't expect to happen. As you can imagine, that's lots of experiences every day, hour and, possibly, minute.

The thalamus receptionist plays an important role in error detection. When a stimulus contacts one of your senses – for example your eyes or nose – the impulse travels to the thalamus where it's received as a primitive sensation.

When the sensation is routine – such as when you see someone you know and like – the thalamus rubber stamps it, and sends it directly up to the boss, the neocortex, for processing. Your neocortex then interprets the sensation in terms of location, intensity, and duration. From there, the cortex sends information down to the amygdala where hormones are released that lead to feelings and behavior.

However, when the sensation is non-routine, threatening, or has just slightly threatening potential, the thalamus bypasses the cortex. It makes a 911 call by sending the sensory signal straight to the amygdala.

The amygdala reacts quickly. Sometimes quick is good. For example, catching a glass before it rolls off a table. More often, though, the amygdala overreacts, and you impulsively say or do something that you later regret. When this happens, there's a feeling of not knowing what came over you.

Dan Goleman (1998) calls this overreaction, "amygdala hijacking," because the amygdala commandeers the neocortex. The amygdala's response takes metabolic energy away from working memory in the executive center, and it uses the energy to keep the senses attuned for danger. When this happens, a person becomes less reflective, more reactive, and unable to think straight.

Amygdala hijacking also results in the release of stress hormones, such as cortisol, that evoke the fight or flight response and stay in the body for several hours (Goleman 1998, 76). You can feel that stress response when you slam on the brakes and just barely avoid an accident. Even though you know you're safe, your body might continue to feel charged up for quite awhile.

PREFRONTAL CORTEX: KEEPING YOUR WITS ABOUT YOU

The good news is that you don't have to stay in a hijacked state. It's possible to

WORK OUT BOX

| MINDFUL BREATHING

Mindful breathing is one of the most basic Mindfulness Practices (MPs), and you can do it anywhere and anytime. These instructions describe silent practice. You can also *notice* your breath during an active workday while you're talking with people, working at your computer, or walking to a meeting.

Like training wheels on a bike, labeling is available if you want some support for maintaining your awareness on the breath. If your awareness of breathing is easily distracted by thoughts, by other sensations like knee pain or shoulder tension, or by some other sensory input, you may use labeling to gently guide your awareness back to the breath. If your mindfulness is strong, however, and you're staying relatively focused on the breath, there's no need to label.

Follow these steps to focus your awareness on breathing.

1. Decide how long you would like to practice silent Mindful Breathing. Set a timer, so that you won't need to keep an eye on the clock. I recommend you begin with five to ten minutes.

2. Find a quiet place where you won't be interrupted. Sit, stand, or lie in a comfortable position. Allow your eyes to look downward or gently close.

3. Take three slow breaths with the exhale a bit longer than the inhale.

4. Let go of the slow breathing and any control over your breath. Allow your breath to find its own natural rhythm.

5. *Notice* the area in your body where you feel the breath most predominantly. You might feel the breath most in your abdomen, chest, nostrils, or some other place in your body. Pick one area, and place your awareness there. Feel your breath move in and out of that area.

6. After feeling the breath in that general area in your body, narrow your awareness to a smaller spot. If you're focusing on your chest or abdomen, narrow your awareness to a spot about the size of a quarter. If you're focusing on your nose, select a spot about the size of a dime where your nostrils meet your upper lip. *Notice* the sensations of breathing in the small spot.

7. When your awareness is distracted by thoughts, sensations, or sounds, you have the option to add labeling. If you're focusing on the abdomen or chest, say silently in the back of your mind, as you inhale, "rising." As you exhale, say "falling." If you're aware of the breath at the nostrils, you can note "in" on the inhale, and "out" on the exhale. If you're feeling the breath in some other part of your body, make up your own one-word labels to describe the movements of the inhale and exhale.

8. Continue to practice Mindful Breathing until your timer beeps. Before you return to your regular activities, spend a few moments noticing if you feel different at the end of mindfulness than when you began. Write in your journal what you *noticed* during this exercise.

minimize the impact of amygdala hijacking by practicing mindfulness. Dr. Richard Davidson, Dr. Jon Kabat-Zinn, and colleagues studied the impact of an eight-week mindfulness training program on healthy employees in a biotech work environment (Davidson et al. 2003, 565). EEG measurements of brain activity showed that the mindfulness practitioners had a significant increase in left-sided anterior activation in the PFC. Left-sided anterior activation is associated with reduced anxiety and negative affect as well as increases in positive affect. People with greater left-sided activation also show faster recovery after negative and/or stressful events (Davidson et al. 2003, 566).

KAREN'S FIELDWORK

Once Karen understood more about her naturally negative mind, she was interested in finding more ways to train it to be a bit calmer. After I explained the instructions in the **MINDFUL BREATHING Work Out Box**, she had a few questions.

> KAREN: When I did labeling before, it was either on the timeframe of my thoughts – "Now" or "Narrative" – or on whom I was thinking about – self or other. I haven't labeled sensations in my body. How will this be different?

> SUZANNE: Good question. The activity of labeling should only be about 10 to 15 percent of your mindfulness effort. The remaining energy should be on feeling the sensations of breathing. See if you can keep your labeling voice gentle and neutral as opposed to loud and demanding. Then labeling can sound like a caring friend rather than a drill sergeant.

> KAREN: Got it. How much silent practice do you recommend? I have a friend who does mindfulness for 30 minutes a day. Should I start there?

> SUZANNE: When people are first experimenting with a silent mindfulness practice, I encourage them to win small, rather than lose big. What's the shortest amount of time that you know for sure you can commit to for, let's say, three days a week?

KAREN: The shortest?! I guess five seconds wouldn't give me much bang. How about ten minutes?

SUZANNE: How about winning even smaller just for the next two weeks. I want it to be so easy that you really enjoy it and want more.

KAREN: Okay, I get it. I need to get out my training wheels and be proud of myself for trying. I know for sure I could do at least three minutes a day. It almost takes that long for my computer to boot up on the company network. Would it work for me to practice first thing in the morning?

SUZANNE: Fantastic idea, Karen.

We agreed that she would use a timer, such as a kitchen timer, at her office. At the end of work each day, she would leave the timer on her chair. This would act as a reminder to turn on her computer, set her timer for three minutes, and practice Mindful Breathing. I asked her to keep a log with the day and time she practiced, adding one or two words about how she felt before and after. She committed to do this three days a week, which allowed for running late or having a breakfast meeting a few days each week. I emailed her a sample log to get her started.

We closed out our conversation by discussing her new insights about negative thinking and reactivity.

SUZANNE: What was most valuable from our conversation that you want to remember?

KAREN: Gosh, there were several things. The most powerful thing I learned was that my negative thinking is not only normal, it evolved that way to keep people alive. The thing I'm still confused about, though, is that I don't really need my amygdala to be so hypersensitive. It's not like I'm on the lookout for lions and tigers and bears.

SUZANNE: You're right. Most of us don't have to be alert for extreme danger. Though, what are some experiences that might feel like a predator to your overly sensitive amygdala?

KAREN: I don't want to sound mean, but in a way, Janice was like a predator. She attacked me at the conference, and my mind has never forgotten. Once bitten, twice shy, or something like that?

SUZANNE: That's a fair analogy. And, if I may ask you to stretch a bit. Whose amygdala at work could possibly perceive you as a threat?

KAREN: Everybody's! No, seriously, I am seeing a stream of faces that have reacted negatively to me: Janice on the plane home from the conference when I told her I was mad, my management team last month when I told them about the 3 percent budget cut, and oh, how about that VP in the conference room when I blurted out, "Hey, that's my seat!" That must have freaked out his amygdala. My secretary, the lab supplier when I make a last minute order change, and oh good grief, my son, Jason! That poor child's amygdala. Every time I yell, "Jason!" up the stairs, his blood pressure probably goes up 20 points.

SUZANNE: You've got it. And, I'm not suggesting that you stop telling the truth or asking for what you want. Simply keep the mind in mind. What does that mean to you?

KAREN: Be aware of the amygdala. And, while I'm at it, of all three layers of the brain. What were they? Reptile, mammal, and executive? I see now how I assume that all of my interactions are from human brain to human brain. But, really, the amygdala in the mammal layer of my brain plays such an important role in my life and work, so it must be doing that in everyone I encounter. I guess I could tone down my volume a bit, so that I don't unnecessarily activate people's amygdala. That's what you mean by intrapersonal and interpersonal attunement. You're asking me to be quiet enough so that I can *listen* and *notice* my mind and everyone else's mind. That way I can more consciously influence my behavior and their behavior. That's what the mindfulness is going to help me do, right? And, you're giving me a tool kit of different kinds of mindfulness practices that I can use in different situations. Oh, this is so cool. I'm starting to get it.

SUZANNE: Yep, you certainly are. Enjoy your insights, and I'll look forward to talking with you in two weeks.

CONCEPTS

- A growing body of research points to a "negativity bias" in the brain.

- The brain has three main sections: cerebrum, cerebellum, and brain stem. The cerebrum has four lobes: frontal, parietal, occipital, and temporal.

- The amygdala, in the temporal lobe, processes emotional reactions such as rage, sexual feelings, and the fear response known as "fight or flight."

- The prefrontal cortex (PFC), in the frontal lobe, is the home of the executive function. It orchestrates thoughts and actions based on internal goals. Mindfulness works via parts of the PFC to calm the reactivity of the amygdala.

PART TWO

DEVELOPING THE THREE MINDSETS: CALM, CONFIDENT, AND POWERFUL LEADERSHIP

This section introduces the three Mind to Lead mindsets – Calm, Confident, and Powerful Leadership – and, how to develop them using the three processes – Mindfulness, Exploration, and Influence. **Chapter 4**, on developing Calm Leadership, encourages you to add mindfulness to your work through simple techniques that take from as little as 10 seconds up to a regular silent practice of ten to 20 minutes a day. **Chapter 5**, on becoming a Confident Leader, demonstrates how to neutralize negative, judgmental thoughts that prevent you from taking effective action. **Chapter 6**, on expressing appropriate Powerful Leadership, teaches you how to communicate clearly in order to motivate the wide variety of people in your organization.

CHAPTER 4

MINDSET 1:
MINDFULNESS TRAINING FOR CALM LEADERS

On our next coaching call, Karen reported good success with her silent mindfulness practice. And, she had great follow-up questions.

SUZANNE: How did your silent practice go, Karen?

KAREN: Really well. I liked it. Did you get my log?

SUZANNE: Yes. You practiced four times the first week and five times the second week. It looks like three minutes just wasn't enough.

KAREN: Three minutes went way too fast. I was just settling in, and the timer would go off. So, I'd set it for another three minutes. Then I switched to setting it for seven or eight minutes from the start. Even that went fast.

SUZANNE: How exciting. Where's your comfort zone today for total practice time?

KAREN: I think ten minutes. If I know I have an early morning meeting, I can leave the house for work a bit early so that I can finish a ten-minute practice period. And, if I can't fit in ten minutes, I can still feel good about doing three minutes.

SUZANNE: Outstanding plan. From your log, it looks like the mindfulness is helping you feel better.

KAREN: Oh, gosh, yes. It's kind of amazing how much calmer I feel. When the timer goes off, I jump right into my to-do list and seem to concentrate better and come up with solutions more easily, at least until lunch. The mindfulness doesn't seem to last all day. Though I do *notice* I'm a little less grumpy when I get home from work. I'm listening to my husband and son a bit better than before. When one of them complains about something, I just imagine his amygdalae as tiny red lights flashing in his brain. It makes me laugh, and I'm less reactive. I'm probably more helpful, too.

SUZANNE: That's clever, Karen. You said that the mindfulness doesn't last all day. Something that helps me regain focus is taking a short break every hour or so to feel my breath for one minute. I call it "Pushing the Reset Button." I'm happy that the mindfulness is developing a sense of calm, a mindset that most leaders want to develop. You mentioned the positive impacts of mindfulness on your behavior. Let's talk in a few minutes about how it's impacted the other three realms, too.

I was referring to the four realms of experience – physical, mental, emotional and behavioral. During both intrapersonal and interpersonal attunement, a mindful leader *notices* what is going on in as many of the realms as possible. In this chapter, you'll learn how tuning into those realms in yourself and others helps to relax and focus your mind.

SUZANNE: First, what questions came up about your silent mindfulness practice?

KAREN: What do I do about thinking? You told me before that hearts beat, and minds think. So, I remembered that having thoughts isn't a problem. Thinking is just something to get used to, right?

SUZANNE: That's right. When you *notice* that you're distracted by a thought, gently bring your awareness back to the breath. Sometimes it's helpful to acknowledge the thinking process. For example, when you *notice* a thought, you can gently label, "thinking about blank," and fill in the blank with a word or two that describes the content of the thought. For example, "thinking about budget" or "thinking about weekend." Then return to feeling the breath.

KAREN: I don't stay on the breath for very long.

SUZANNE: That's normal. Mindfulness is as much about the "coming back" as the "staying on." There are three basic skills within mindfulness practice: aiming, sustaining, and redirecting awareness. How did you see those at work in your practice over the last two weeks?

KAREN: Let's see. I aimed my awareness on the breathing sensations in my abdomen. I tried to sustain my attention on them. And, when I *noticed* that my awareness was distracted by a thought or sound or something else, I redirected my awareness back to the sensations. Is that it?

SUZANNE: Perfect. Sometimes beginners think that mindfulness practice should only be about aim and sustain, and that something is wrong when the mind is distracted. The distractions, noticing the distractions, and redirecting back to the object of mindfulness – in your case, the breath – are all equal parts of the practice. How well does that answer your question about thinking?

KAREN: A little bit. It covers some situations, though not all. There were a couple days when I sat down, set my timer, and my mind was racing. I was so jumpy that it was hard to sit still. I ended up getting really frustrated, because I was trying to force myself to be calm and feel my breath. I hate to say this, Suzanne, but it was awful. It made me want to quit mindfulness. Sometimes being calm just doesn't work.

SUZANNE: You're right, Karen. As one of my friends says, "'Calm is overrated." We don't have to be calm all the time to be effective. And, forcing ourselves to be calm doesn't work – it's not calming – particularly when the mind or body is really revved up. This seems like a good time to talk about the four realms.

THE FOUR REALMS OF EXPERIENCE

To explain the realms, I told Karen about one of my clients, David, a small business owner. David was a high energy, 30-something entrepreneur with his hands in numerous high tech and artistic projects. He was action-oriented and rarely had trouble motivating himself. However, he was becoming increasingly frustrated with himself for procrastinating on an important purchase for one of his businesses.

In order to grow his business, he needed to buy several high-end microphones. Yet, every time he was about to call the supplier, he got upset, talked himself out of it, and started doing some other task. The procrastination was bugging him.

For many of us, the most apparent realm of experience is behavior. It's relatively easy to *notice* our actions and other people's actions. However, when a leader is having trouble understanding his behavior on the outside, it can be helpful to *notice* what's happening on the inside – the physical, mental, and emotional realms – and how those factors contribute to the problem.

The easiest inner sphere for most of my clients to access is the mental realm, which we experience through thoughts. When I asked David to write his thoughts about buying the equipment, his list included a variety of thoughts – some positive and some negative:

- "This will sink us into even more debt."
- "I don't like the supplier."
- "We could sell the microphones at a great profit."
- "My business partner will get upset."
- "I need to take this risk. It's good for the business."

Looking at the list helped him understand how his thoughts pulled him in different directions thus immobilizing his behavior.

To uncover the next inner realm – emotional – I asked how he felt about the situation.

DAVID: Lousy.

SUZANNE: That sounds accurate. When I feel lousy, it's often because there are several different emotions, sort of like the conflicting thoughts you have about the mikes.

DAVID: What do you mean?

SUZANNE: Does the thought, "This will sink us into even more debt" reflect a different emotion than the thought, "I don't like the supplier"?

DAVID: I guess I'm scared about the debt and angry at the supplier. He's promised us delivery dates in the past that just don't happen.

SUZANNE: Yes. How about emotions associated with profit, your partner, and risk?

DAVID: I'm excited about the potential profit, worried about my partner's reaction, and definitely scared about the risk. I get it. The thoughts and feelings are all mixed up together. It seems like thoughts and feelings are similar. Or, what's the difference? Is there a difference?

I could see that David was getting a little confused. The link between thoughts and feelings is consistent with what scientists are learning about the brain. Paul Ekman and his colleagues (Ekman et al. 2005, 59) report this finding from Davidson and Irwin (1999): "Every region in the brain that has been identified with some aspect of emotion has also been identified with aspects of cognition." This means that, according to scientists, the neural circuitry of feelings is related to the circuitry of thoughts. I take the linking even further. Because I define an emotion as a combination of thoughts and associated body sensations, all three of the inner realms – sensations, thoughts, and feelings – are related. I shared this with David.

DAVID: Hold it. Slow down. What do you mean by body sensations? Where did that come from?

SUZANNE: Let's try this. Get an image in your mind of someone you care about deeply. Now pretend that this person just walked into the room. Can you see that in your mind?

DAVID: Yes, I've got it.

SUZANNE: Stay with that experience for a few moments. Your reaction to this person could be called the emotion "love." Love includes body sensations and associated thoughts about the person. What thoughts and body sensations did you experience?

DAVID: There were several thoughts, like, "What a cool person, I'm really lucky to know her, I love hanging out with her." And, body sensations?! Let's not go there, Suzanne!

SUZANNE (Laughing): How about above your waist, David?

DAVID: My chest feels warm. And, now I'm blushing. Okay, I get it. A feeling – in the emotional realm – is a combination of thoughts – mental realm – and body sensations – physical realm. So what?

SUZANNE: I call that the Inner Soup. What goes on inside us directly impacts our behavior outside. How's that true with the mikes?

DAVID: I'll call it the Inner Goop. I'm immobilized by it. I can't make the call. How does being aware of the Goop make a differ-ence?

Noticing the so-called Inner Goop and our outer behavior affects us in two ways. First, the mind is like a toggle switch that has only two settings: narrative or pres-ent moment. The narrative – or storytelling setting – can be very stressful. It's when the mind is in a monologue about either the past or the future. Noticing any or all of the four realms switches the toggle to the present moment setting, stops the stressful narrative, and allows us to accept to some degree whatever is going on, even if it's unpleasant.

I asked David to *notice* what happened to the stressful narrative when he toggled back to the present moment setting. He said the narrative setting was like having different voices in his head arguing about whether he should buy the mikes or not. Writing the thoughts down and naming the feelings did stop the story and calmed him down. It also let him see the story, almost like he was watching a movie about himself.

Watching a movie about yourself is a good analogy. Noticing your experience in the present moment slows or stops the narrative. Describing, or labeling – any of the four realms – can calm the mind, because it has been shown to reduce neural firing in the amygdala. (See **LABELING EMOTIONS Mind Trick Box**.)

In order to experience how the physical realm is linked to the mental and emotional realms, I asked David to close his eyes and play a video in his mind of him thinking about the microphones. He could see himself in his office, thinking about calling the supplier, getting confused and reactive, changing his mind, and doing something else. As he was playing the video, I asked David to move his awareness from his mind into his body. He placed his awareness at the top of his head, and moved it down through his body as he "looked" for strong sensations.

He noticed a ball of tension in his abdomen; it was the size of a cantaloupe and felt heavy and dense. I asked him to start on one side of the melon, and move his awareness through it to the other side while scanning for the hot spot – the most uncomfortable place in the sensation. When he found the hot spot, he described it as rigid and dark. I asked him to move his awareness into the dark spot and simply *notice* the sensations.

David gently kept his awareness on the tension's hot spot. After 30 seconds of silence, I asked what was happening. He said the hot spot had disappeared. How about the whole melon? He could still feel it, though the sensations had lessened and weren't uncomfortable any more.

For a first try at mindfulness of the physical realm, David displayed a lot of skill and experienced a significant reduction in discomfort. This doesn't always happen when a person focuses on an unpleasant sensation. However, in my experience of leading people through this exercise, the sensation lessens or dissolves about 75 percent of the time.

MIND TRICK BOX
| LABELING EMOTIONS

Talk therapies are based on the principle that you can manage emotional upset by expressing, or labeling, your feelings. Neuroscientists wondered if that theory was true, and if so, what happens in the brain during labeling.

To study labeling, Matt Lieberman and his colleagues at UCLA showed emotionally upsetting images to subjects, and then asked the subjects to perform a variety of tasks (Lieberman et al. 2007, 423). While the subjects performed the tasks, the scientists conducted functional MRI scans to see which parts of the brain were working. For example, the subjects saw an image of a woman scowling with the words, "scared" and "angry" underneath her picture. Subjects were asked to choose which word best described the scowling woman. (I'm going with "angry." How about you?)

Results showed that labeling the emotion decreased activity in the amygdala (less fight/flight) and increased activity in the right ventrolateral prefrontal cortex (more emotion regulation) (Lieberman et al. 2007, 426).

In a similar study at UCLA, David Creswell and colleagues (Creswell et al. 2007, 560) had the subjects take a mindfulness assessment before subjects looked at the upsetting pictures. Results showed that the subjects with higher levels of mindfulness had greater prefrontal cortical activation and reduced amygdala activity during labeling (Creswell et al. 2007, 562).

These studies showed that labeling an intense emotion lowers neural firing in the limbic system more than simply observing an emotion in a photo without describing it. The second study showed that people with a foundation of mindfulness have even less limbic firing and more prefrontal regulation than people without mindfulness.

After noticing his thoughts, feelings, and body sensations, we returned to his list of thoughts. I helped David investigate the most stressful thought, "This will sink us into even more debt." Exploring the thought helped him see rationally that he couldn't be certain the microphones would lead to more debt. (In **Chapter 5**, I'll show you how to investigate and possibly neutralize negative thoughts.) By the end of our call, David had regained his confidence and decided definitively to invest in the microphones. In an email later that day, he said that he had talked with his partner, called the supplier, and ordered the microphones. He was happy with himself and the results he got.

MIND TRICK BOX
| UNPLEASANT BODY SENSATIONS

While it might sound scary to go there, nobody dies from noticing an unpleasant sensation. Like David's stomach tension, the uncomfortable pangs and twinges in your body are simply neural firings. Not only are they not going to kill you, they might be sending valuable messages that something needs your attention. For example, when you're about to ask for a raise, you could think of that queasiness in your stomach as a message – "This is important and exciting!" – rather than as something irritating or embarrassing.

If David's experience made you curious about unpleasant sensations, try the Body Scan or Sensation Scan in Appendix III. *Notice* all of your sensations – pleasant, unpleasant, and neutral – without trying to change or ignore them.

If you're hesitant to feel unpleasant sensations in your body, then trust that instinct and don't start there. Instead, when you're feeling uncomfortable or distressed, simply feel your feet on the floor or your seat in the chair. If that helps you feel more relaxed, you might want to try slowly moving your awareness to the edge of an uncomfortable sensation and briefly "touching" it. Whenever you want to go back to the relaxing, safe sensations, simply return your awareness to your feet or seat. Over time, it might feel safe to move your awareness further into the uncomfortable sensation, and experience it for a while. Only do this when you're ready.

Write in your journal what you noticed during this exercise.

THE FOUR FOUNDATIONS OF CALM

After I told David's story, Karen understood the connections among the four realms.

> KAREN: When my mind is racing, my body, emotions, and behavior are probably racing, too. So, sitting still and watching my breath isn't going to work very well. Does that mean I should skip mindfulness on those days?

> SUZANNE: Not necessarily. What did you learn from David's experience that might be a substitute for silent breath awareness?

> KAREN: I could write down my thoughts. That was one of the first

exercises you gave me. Or, I guess I look for hot spots in my body or label my emotions. Oh, there are loads of things I can do other than watch my breath. Do those count as mindfulness practice?

SUZANNE: Absolutely. I'll send you a list of Mindfulness Practices (MPs). (See Appendix III.) It's a collection of simple awareness techniques that help mindful leaders let go of the narrative, come into the present moment, and develop a calm mindset even in the most challenging situations. Of course, the MPs work much better if you've already developed a baseline foundation of calm. Almost anyone can learn techniques that relax him pretty quickly. However, if he doesn't have a relatively healthy lifestyle with some ongoing investment in appreciating and practicing calm, it'll be more like starting from scratch every time he does the practices.

KAREN: That makes sense. One of our lab techs drinks six or seven diet colas a day. And, he can't figure out why he's so wired all the time. You're saying that watching my breath 10 minutes a day won't be a panacea; I need to take care of my health in other ways.

SUZANNE: Exactly. When I speak to large audiences, I often teach a very simple MP called Feet & Seat. You can try it now. Feel the bottom of your feet in contact with the floor and the back of your body in contact with the chair. Because it's very easy to learn, most people, even those who've never done mindfulness or relaxation techniques, will relax immediately.

KAREN: Wow, yes, it feels great. I feel heavy and relaxed.

SUZANNE: While almost everyone feels some benefit from their first try at Feet & Seat – they enter a *state* of calm – the people who experience the best results with mindfulness are those who make a commitment to practice on a regular basis. Over time, they develop an enduring *trait* of being calm. Research has shown this to be true, particularly in long-term meditation practitioners. (See **LONG-TERM MEDITATION Mind Trick Box**).

MIND TRICK BOX
| LONG-TERM MEDITATION PRACTICE

Neuroscientist Dr. Richard Davidson's lab has conducted controlled studies on the impact of meditation on brain activity. Davidson's colleague, Antoine Lutz, placed 128 electrodes on eight Tibetan monks with more than 10,000 hours of meditation experience and asked them to meditate on "unconditional loving-kindness and compassion" (Lutz et al. 2004, 16369). Their EEGs showed brain waves oscillating at roughly 40 cycles per second. Such gamma waves are usually difficult to see, but the monks' were easily visible and indicated highly focused thought and insights. The EEG also showed synchronized oscillations, a phenomenon that sometimes occurs in patients under anesthesia.

Lutz's team compared the monks' EEGs to a control group of college students with no meditation experience. The monks produced gamma waves that were 30 times stronger than the students'. In addition, larger areas of the meditators' brains were active, including the left prefrontal cortex, which is responsible for positive emotions (Lutz et al. 2004, 16372).

Even without investing 10,000 hours, a regular mindfulness practice can develop the beneficial facets of nonreactivity, nonjudging, and actaware.

Karen understood the difference and said she was interested in an overall calm checkup, sort of like the safety inspection a mechanic does on your car once a year.

I referred her to two assessments. The Calm Leader Assessment on my website (themindtolead.com) is a brief analysis of your calm foundation in each of the four realms. For example, under physical calm, there are items about diet and exercise. The behavioral calm section includes items about time management and delegation.

The other tool is the Early Warning Signals Assessment (See *Appendix II*). It's a checklist of physical, mental, emotional, and behavioral signs that indicate you could be getting out of balance. This list helps your **Reporter** be on the lookout for ways that your body, mind, heart, and actor – that's what I call the part of you in charge of the behavioral realm – are beginning to exit the calm zone. As you learn to *notice* these signs in yourself through intrapersonal attunement, you might also become more attuned to reading similar cues in others.

When Karen asked about the difference between physical and behavioral calm, I explained that physical calm is your inner body experience that no one else can see or hear from the outside. Behavioral calm is what others can see.

There are lots of ways to bring awareness and calm to our behavior at work and in our personal lives. David Allen's book, *Getting Things Done* (Allen, 2001), has several strategies that help increase mental and behavioral calm. I highly recommend it. You also might want to try the Behavioral MP: Right Now I'm... (See *Appendix III*).

Before we finished, I asked Karen to return briefly to my question about how her mindfulness practice impacted the four realms.

> KAREN: Oh, right. I felt physical relaxation, mental focus on tasks, emotional balance or openness to others, I'm not sure what to call that, and behavioral....let's see, behavioral decisiveness or deliberateness. Again, I'm not sure what to call it. Gee, that's a lot of benefits, isn't it?

> SUZANNE: It is. Your list is similar to the findings by **Ruth Baer** (Baer et al. 2006, 30). They identified three traits of mindfulness that help people feel better: nonreactivity to inner experience, nonjudging of experience, and acting with awareness, which they shortened to actaware. Actaware is what you're referring to as behavioral deliberateness.

> KAREN: I like that word, actaware. And, I'd agree that I was less reactive and a little less judgmental, though I wouldn't go so far as to say I'm at nonjudging yet.

> SUZANNE: You're skillful at self-reflection, Karen. Not all leaders are this good at observing their inner experience. And, you shared valuable insights on our call today. What are you committing to do before our next conversation?

> KAREN: I want to continue my silent mindfulness practice for at least 10 minutes three times a week, complete the two assessments you mentioned, review the list of MPs that you're going to send, and buy David Allen's book. Thanks for your help. This is all making sense. I feel like I've come a long way since our first conversation two months ago.

WORK OUT BOX
| MANAGING YOUR TIME

My best advice for handling your to-do list is to read David Allen's book *Getting Things Done* (Allen 2001). He's got a unique, brain-based approach to thinking about and managing time. David's techniques for cataloging your thoughts and action steps will organize the desktop in your mind and help you stay in the present moment. He explains why you don't need to spend time thinking about anything except what you're doing right now. Simply keep paper and pen with you all the time so that you can write down ideas right away. Once your mind sees the idea captured on paper, you'll stop thinking about it and refocus on your current task.

THE MINDFULNESS STEPS AND TOOLS

The Mind to Lead model cultivates three mindsets – calm, confident, and power – by using three processes – Mindfulness, Exploration, and Influence. To help you develop the three processes, I created three simple steps and a collection of tools for each one. For example, the Mindfulness Steps, **Notice - Breathe - Allow,** develop the mindfulness process that over time cultivates a mindset of calm. The Mindfulness Tools are nine practices to use in a variety of silent and active settings. You can apply some practices for as little as a few seconds to quickly experience a sense of calm. A longer application of five to 30 minutes on a regular basis will give you even greater benefits. Remember that the steps and tools build on the calm foundation that you're developing and maintaining by using the life and work style upgrades in the Calm Leader Assessment (themindtolead.com).

THE MINDFULNESS STEPS: NOTICE - BREATHE - ALLOW

The Leadership Attunement Model (Figure 4.1) shows how to use the Mindfulness Steps – **Notice - Breathe - Allow** – in two contexts: with "Self" and "Other." Apply the Mindfulness Steps to attune with yourself, to attune with the other person, or to help the other person be calm. These options include:

- Calm yourself while solo
- Calm yourself while reacting to the other person
- Calm yourself while reading the other person
- Calm the other person

FIGURE 4.1 LEADERSHIP ATTUNEMENT MODEL: CALM LEADER

MINDSET	CALM
PROCESS	Mindfulness
STEPS	
SELF	• **NOTICE** what is happening for me physically, mentally, emotionally, and behaviorally. • **BREATHE.** • **ALLOW** what is happening for me even if it's uncomfortable.
OTHER	• **NOTICE** what I hypothesize is happening for the other person physically, mentally, emotionally, and behaviorally. • **BREATHE.** • **ALLOW** what is happening for the other person even if it's uncomfortable for either/both of us.
TOOLS	• Feet & Seat • Mindful Breathing • Now or Narrative
For six more Mindfulness Practices, see Appendix III	

CALM YOURSELF WHILE SOLO

Use the three steps to calm yourself when you're alone. At any time during the day, take a few moments to *notice, breathe,* and *allow* your experience in any of the four realms:

• **PHYSICAL**: Do a brief Body Scan or Sensation Scan (See *Appendix III*). *Notice* the sensations. Take a few breaths into your whole body or into each of the strong sensations. *Allow* the sensations to feel as they are – comfortable, uncomfortable, or neutral – without trying to change or ignore them.

• **MENTAL**: *Notice* your thoughts by writing them on a piece of paper. Take a few breaths with the exhales longer than the inhales. *Allow* your thoughts to be as they are – even for just a few moments – without wanting to change them.

• **EMOTIONAL**: *Notice* your feelings by labeling them aloud or writing them on a piece of paper. You might want to separate each feeling into its two parts – the sensations and the thoughts. Take a few deep breaths with the exhales longer than the inhales. *Allow* your feelings to be as they are without wanting – even for just a few moments – to change them.

• **BEHAVIORAL**: Recall a situation when you either regretted your behavior or were proud of it. Replay a video in your mind of yourself in that situation. *Notice* your actions and whether each was something (1) inappropriate that you did like yelling at an employee, (2) appropriate that you neglected to do like have a difficult conversation, or (3) appropriate that you did like affirming your team's ability to work well together. Take a few breaths with the exhales longer than the inhales. *Allow* your actions to be as they were without wanting – even for just a few moments – for them to be different.

CALM YOURSELF WHILE REACTING TO THE OTHER PERSON

As you become more skilled at calming yourself when you're alone, you'll be able to use the Mindfulness Steps to calm yourself when you're with others – even the most challenging people in your work and life. The three steps will help you feel more relaxed and in control of your behavior.

To get a sense of how to use the three steps with another person, take a few moments right now to calm yourself using **Notice - Breathe - Allow**. Next, think of a difficult person you work with. I'll refer to this person as Pat. I'll guide you through the three steps as you play a video in your mind of an unpleasant interaction that you had with Pat. Once you learn this process, you can use the three steps in real time with both pleasant and unpleasant people.

As you see yourself talking with Pat on the phone or in person, *notice* how you're reacting physically. Where do you feel discomfort in your body? Move your awareness into the strongest sensation. Take a breath, and *allow* the physical discomfort in that sensation or your body as a whole.

What thoughts and emotions are you having? *Notice* two or three thoughts and feelings that you're experiencing. If you're having trouble identifying your feelings, review the Feelings List in Appendix I. Take a breath, and *allow* any mental or emotional discomfort.

Return to the video, and *notice* your behavior; how are you acting with Pat? Are you interacting in an authentic way that includes him/her in the conversation? Or, are you interrupting, ignoring, or tuning Pat out in some way? Perhaps you're feeling intimidated, and you're letting Pat control the conversation. Take another breath, and *allow* your behavior to be what it is even if you wish you were acting differently.

Whatever you're sensing, thinking, feeling, or doing, it's okay. Simply **Notice - Breathe - Allow**. Even if it feels very uncomfortable, *allow* your experience to be the way it is. Using your prefrontal cortex to label your experience while it's happening in the present moment – or even in a video replay after an experience – can reduce the firing of the amygdala. Bringing your experience into awareness may lessen the negative impacts of it.

Even though the experience with Pat might seem mostly unpleasant, take a few moments to also *notice* one or two things that are going well in the experience. It's helpful to see the whole picture and realize that some aspects of it are working.

CALM YOURSELF WHILE READING THE OTHER PERSON

A third option for using the Mindfulness Steps is to shift your attention from yourself to Pat. This option is called, "Hypothesis about Another." As you play the video, *notice* any cues about Pat's physical, mental, emotional, or behavioral realms. *Breathe* as you create a thumbnail sketch of Pat's experience in your mind, and *allow* Pat to be as he/she is. In addition to noticing any unpleasant aspects, see if you can also be aware of neutral or even pleasant aspects about Pat. You can *notice*, for example:

- **PHYSICALLY**: Do the face, hands, and whole body appear relatively tense or relaxed?
- **MENTALLY**: What issues or opinions could be prominent in his/her mind?
- **EMOTIONALLY**: Combine your observations about the physical state and your guess about the mental state to select one of the four basic emotional states: mad, sad, glad or afraid. If possible, narrow your choice down to a more specific emotion using the Feelings List in Appendix I. Remember, it's common for people to experience two or three different emotions at one time.
- **BEHAVIORALLY**: How is the person acting, particularly his/her speech? Is the person talking a lot or very little? What does the tone of voice convey? Is he/she talking mostly about people issues or more about a task?

If you're observing someone you don't like, it's common to react negatively to this scanning process. If your experience becomes very unpleasant, return to feeling your own inner experience using **Notice - Breathe - Allow**.

By the way, the two reasons that I don't train leaders how to read very specific nonverbal cues are, one, I'm not an expert at nonverbals, and two, you already know intuitively how to read those cues to some extent. I believe that not all, but most, sighted people have a natural instinct for reading other people's physical cues. You can probably determine if a person is mad, sad, glad, afraid, or some combination. If you think you need help or you're curious about learning the science of facial expressions, read Paul Ekman's book, *Emotions Revealed: Recognizing Faces and Feelings to Improve Communication and Emotional Life* (Ekman 2007).

One more point about picking up cues from people. I've heard from visually impaired people that they feel they have a heightened sense of hearing and can read people via subtleties in the voice. If you're visually impaired, create your hypothesis based on signals from senses other than seeing.

Remember that you're forming a hypothesis, also known as an assumption or theory. Avoid becoming attached to your theory about what's going on for Pat, because you could be wrong. For example, there's a psychological process called projection, when the unconscious mind ascribes one's own personal thoughts, feelings, or impulses, especially undesirable ones, to someone else. For example, if you're already angry at Pat, you might hypothesize that Pat is angry, because you're projecting that emotion from your mind onto Pat. Forming a theory is valuable; just don't confuse it with the facts of what the other person is experiencing, which you won't know until you ask.

CALM THE OTHER PERSON: DAVID'S CASE STUDY

Once you can calm yourself while you're reading the other person, you might feel confident to share some of that calm. The week after I taught David, the young entrepreneur, about **Notice – Breathe – Allow**, he told me how he used it to help calm one of his marketing reps, Lesley.

The day after they learned that a potential client chose one of their competitors for a huge project, Lesley walked into David's office and plopped down in a chair with a huff. She rolled her eyes and blurted out, "I can't believe they went with Ace."

At first, David's natural inclination was to appease her and say something like, "Forget about it. We'll get the next one. Ace had an in. We didn't have a chance anyway." He also thought about telling her off with, "You blew a really big chance for us."

The hardest comeback for David to let go of was to not turn the conversation into being about him with something like, "Yeah, I'm mad, too. I ran into the CEO at the gym the day before they decided, and he made a snarky comment about how there was stiff competition, and we better be on our best game. He knew the whole thing was wired, and we didn't have a chance. What a jerk."

Fortunately, David realized that pacifying or shaming Lesley, or trash talking the client wasn't going to take their conversation to a new level, to a place where she hadn't already been in her own mind. He described to me how his job was to help Lesley learn from the situation and then to move the conversation to a solution.

David told me he was glad that we had just talked about the three Mindfulness Steps. Instead of responding to Lesley right away, he paused for a couple seconds of intrapersonal attunement. He did a quick NBA – that's what he calls **Notice - Breathe - Allow** – for how he was feeling. It calmed him down, and he remembered that as her boss, the conversation was about Lesley, not him. Then, he took just a couple more seconds for interpersonal attunement – to NBA what appeared to be happening for Lesley without expecting or wanting her to change. He remembered that when I told him that he could do all of this in a few seconds, he didn't believe me. But, he said the practice proved me right. He quickly came up with a hypothesis of what she was experiencing. He used the Facts & Feelings tool and said to her: "It sounds like you're angry about the proposal being turned down. Is that what's going on?"

David gave me some more background. He had known Lesley for years. They went to college together and had an honest relationship. She wasn't intimidated about him being her boss. So, she told him the truth, "No, I'm not angry. Well, okay, you're sort of right, I'm angry. Not at them. At me! I didn't do enough research on the client or spend enough time on the proposal. Mostly I feel embarrassed."

David felt excited when she said that. He could watch her take in his hypothesis about being angry – it gave her something to react to – and digest it, like she was slightly buying it but it wasn't the whole story. In order to respond to him, she went inside herself to *notice* what was happening. Then, he continued with the other Mindfulness Steps.

> DAVID: Lesley, let's just take a breath for a second. This is disappointing. Can we just *allow* that?
>
> LESLEY (taking a breath and relaxing): You're right. It's not the end of the world. What can I do differently to get the buy the next time?

DAVID: It sounds like you're concerned that you didn't do enough research or refine the proposal. Let's decide what you can change next time and at what points you will check in with me for feedback on the proposal.

Lesley felt confident that she could put her new action plan to work right away. David was pleasantly surprised that what started out as a challenging conversation turned into a proactive planning session. They ended the conversation by making a list of what Lesley had been doing well. When he finished telling me the story, I asked what he most wanted to remember from the experience.

DAVID: Throughout my "scan, hypothesize, and reflect" process, it's important that I stay calm. I was a little nervous to use the Facts & Feelings tool. If she had been resistant to that reflective feedback, I would have had to really focus myself to not get pulled into her emotions. I used NBA to maintain my neutral observer status.

SUZANNE: It was value added for Lesley when you let go of your story so easily and focused on her experience. Can you also see situations like this in the future, when it would be appropriate either sometime later in the conversation or on another day, to share your own frustration and what you learned from it?

DAVID: I did that a little bit when we talked about solutions. I told Lesley that I was frustrated with the short turnaround time on the proposal though I never told the client that. I committed to Lesley that, in the future, I would contact a client immediately when I felt the proposal deadline was unfair.

In summary, the Mindfulness Steps – **Notice - Breathe - Allow** (NBA) – can take as little as a few seconds. When you're alone, do the steps to internally attune with yourself. When you're with another person, you can use the steps in three different ways:

- Calm yourself while reacting to the other person
- Calm yourself while reading the other person
- Calm the other person

"Reacting to" and "reading" the other have subtle differences. "Reacting to the other" refers to your initial internal response to making contact with the other person. Using intrapersonal attunement, you *notice* what it's like for you to initially experience the other person, perhaps when you see that you received an email from her in your inbox, hear her voice on the phone, or see her face. Even though you might have a mixture of thoughts and feelings, in general, your reaction will usually have a positive, negative, or neutral charge. There's no need to judge or try to change the charge. Simply **Notice - Breathe - Allow**.

"Reading the other" is more interactive and uses interpersonal attunement. After you acknowledge your immediate "reaction to" the other and calm yourself, then you can get curious and shift your focus to her. Do a five-second scan of her physical, mental, emotional, and behavioral cues to generate a theory. Calm yourself. Then, you're ready to communicate and possibly help calm her.

CASE STUDY: WHEN REACTING TO THE OTHER FEELS TOO GOOD

So far, I've emphasized how to calm yourself in response to negative stimuli. Let's not overlook positive stimuli in the workplace. Some of your colleagues are good-looking or just plain enjoyable to be around. Human attraction is a wonderful thing, as long as you can respond in an appropriate way. While the alcohol industry wants you to, "Drink responsibly," I encourage you to, "Enjoy attractive people responsibly."

This is a long story that I'll try to condense. When I was married, I was very attracted to one of my clients, George. He was hot-looking, really smart, and passionate about his work. Thanks to my mindfulness practice, I was able to *notice* when I was lusting after him via my thoughts, body sensations (hard to ignore those!), and emotions. To help me be transparent about my feelings, I told my husband about the attraction. This didn't make the thoughts or sensations go away, but it did reduce my guilt. And, it deepened the honesty in our relationship.

I hoped all of this awareness and honesty would dampen my attraction to George; unfortunately, it didn't. I sort of became obsessed with him. I never told him about it, but the obsession continued for many months, until something wonderful happened. I ran into George at a meeting and gave him a long, inappropriate hug. He looked stunned, and I felt embarrassed and ashamed. I realized that something needed to change and that I had to control myself, so that I didn't act out any more. I couldn't go on like this.

When I got home from the meeting, I knew that beating myself up about the hug wasn't helping, so I decided to take a different approach. I got curious. Instead of watching my experience and being mindful of my sensations, thoughts, feelings, and actions, I investigated what George meant to me. I asked myself, "What does George have that I want?" I didn't mean sexually. I meant literally, "What does George have that I envy and want in my own life?"

The answers came quickly. He was a good-looking, successful renegade. Admired in his field, innovative, funny, fit, a great dancer, and a published author. The list went on and on. It sounds too easy, but as my envy became clear, I realized, "Oh, it's not that I *want* George, it's that I want to *be* George. " You probably won't believe this, but this single, simple insight brought a huge smile to my face, and I immediately relaxed.

Of course, this insight didn't completely eliminate my desire for George. I still thought about him. Thankfully, though, as my envy surfaced more in my awareness, my desire eventually disappeared.

Years later, I read a straightforward explanation of the power of envy. I highly recommend psychoanalyst Norberto Keppe's book, *The Origin of Illness: Psychological, Physical and Social* (Keppe 2002). He sees envy as the fundamental human problem. Because envy makes us lose contact with ourselves and reality, it blocks our own motivation and action. Obsessing about George wasted the energy that I wanted to put into making my own life wonderful. Once I understood my envy, who needed George? I learned to dance and wrote this book.

In summary, it's normal to be attracted to people at work. However, before attraction escalates to distraction or concern, use the Mindfulness Steps to explore what's happening inside you. And, seek out other ways to handle strong attraction such as individual or couples therapy or talking with a religious leader. There's lots of good support available to stop the stress of over-attraction.

THE MINDFULNESS TOOLS

I refer to the Mindfulness Tools as Mindfulness Practices or MPs. The nine MPs in Appendix III are organized according to the four foundations: physical, mental, emotional, and behavioral.

Because there are so many good resources about other well-known mindfulness practices like yoga, tai chi, and other forms of prayer or meditation, I didn't include them in Appendix III. All of those practices are excellent ways to strengthen your mindfulness and calm yourself. If you're already doing one or more of them, keep it up. If you're curious about trying any of those, please take a class, read a book, or rent a DVD.

After you've experimented with using the MPs in your work and life, you'll invent new ways to be mindful. I love hearing how people have adapted and created new practices. Please email your ideas to me via themindtolead.com.

Now that you understand the benefits of mindfulness and how to bring your awareness into the present moment when you're alone or with people, let's look at what to do about extremely stressful or judgmental thoughts.

CONCEPTS

- To stay calm, leaders can build a healthy foundation in four areas: physically, mentally, emotionally, and behaviorally.

- The Mindfulness Steps of **NOTICE - BREATHE - ALLOW** (NBA) bring your awareness into the present moment and promote further calm in each of the four realms. You can use the Mindfulness Steps in four different ways to (a) calm yourself while solo, (b) calm yourself while reacting to the other person, (c) calm yourself while reading the other person, and (d) calm the other person.

- The Mindfulness Practices in Appendix III can be used in a silent practice or during your workday interactions. You can practice them either for brief periods to immediately put you in a calm state, or they can be done regularly over months and years to build a calm trait.

CHAPTER 5

MINDSET 2:
EXPLORATION TRAINING FOR CONFIDENT LEADERS

A few days after our last call, I got an email from Karen. She was frustrated with one of her managers, Mark, and was finding herself increasingly reactive to him in meetings and even emails. Karen wrote that Mark had been struggling for several months to hold one of his direct reports accountable for a challenging task. I suggested that we have a quick check-in conversation in the next 24 hours.

KAREN: Thanks for being available on short notice, Suzanne.

SUZANNE: I'm happy to help. Would you like to try the laser coaching format that I've mentioned before?

KAREN: Forgive me, what's that again?

SUZANNE: The brain likes simple messages. A **Laser Message** is 12 words or less. It helps the sender and receiver *focus* on what's most important. We don't have to count the words. Sticking with one sentence is enough of a goal. You want to try it?

KAREN: Sure. I'll start. One of my managers, Mark, isn't holding his assistant accountable for running the payroll.

SUZANNE: What are your reactions in the four realms?

KAREN: Tension in my forehead and throat, thoughts like "He's not strong enough," and "I don't know what to do about it," emotions are angry, sad, overwhelmed. Sorry, I know I'm going over one sentence. And, what's the fourth one? Oh, actions. I'm short with Mark, I'm tense and short with him, saying things like, "Fix this, Mark," without really trying to help him.

SUZANNE: Good work. How can I help?

KAREN: One sentence is hard. Just a moment, let me think…I want help for me to stay calm with him, and frankly, I was wondering if you could coach him. He has a very challenging employee issue.

SUZANNE: I want to help you feel confident to help him feel confident to help his employee.

KAREN: After trying to help Mark for months, my confidence is at an all-time low; he probably feels that way, too.

SUZANNE: How do you experience low confidence?

KAREN: This must be the realms again. Uh, let's see…slumped shoulders, "I don't know what to do, I'm a lousy boss," self-loathing, sadness, and after I push Mark for a while and it doesn't work, then I avoid him.

SUZANNE: How have you or could you use the MPs to help?

KAREN: I'm doing my silent practice, and I've been trying to do **Notice - Breathe - Allow** when I talk with him, but it's hard to *allow* my negative thoughts about him and me. They're painful and immobilizing.

SUZANNE: I'm sorry it's so difficult, Karen. Keep using NBA as much as you can. When your thoughts are very negative, remember that writing them down helped in the past. You might want to try that again. On our next call, I'd like to share the second Mind to Lead process, Exploration. May I send you a link to my Confident Leader Assessment (themindtolead.com) and a brief worksheet developed by Byron Katie to fill out?

KAREN: Yes, and I'll get them back to you before we talk next Tuesday. I feel better just noticing and labeling what's going on. Thanks.

SUZANNE: I'm glad you're feeling better. You're doing well with the mindfulness. There'll always be good and bad stuff coming and going in our work and life. Success with The Mind to Lead model is more about the *internal process* of noticing experience, and less about the *external content* of managing experience, which is guaranteed to be a constantly changing stream of pleasant, unpleasant, and neutral.

THE RISKS IN BELIEVING OUR THOUGHTS

You'd never know it by looking at them, however many successful leaders are plagued by self-doubting thoughts. Their lack of confidence isn't due to poor performance in the outer world, but to self-judgment in the inner world. They have trouble appreciating their own achievements. No matter what they accomplish, it's never enough. Some are afflicted with self-loathing that undermines their confidence. For people with this type of self-judgment, working harder or longer hours doesn't bring relief or self-assurance, because it's not about what they're doing. It's about what they're thinking.

For some reason, simply because a thought occurs, many people assume that it's true. A mindful leader shouldn't believe his thoughts any more than he should believe everything he reads or hears. When he reads or hears something that doesn't sound right, the natural inclination is to investigate it to find out the truth. That's what I encourage leaders to do with stressful thoughts particularly those that erode confidence like, "I'm not good enough" and so many others. (See Core Leader Beliefs that Erode Confidence).

CORE LEADER BELIEFS THAT ERODE CONFIDENCE

Some of the core negative beliefs that erode leader confidence.

- I'm not good enough.
- I don't know what to do.
- They shouldn't have selected me for this job.
- I should resign and go back to my technical job.

- Leading is too hard.
- Leading is a thankless job.
- Nobody understands the position I'm in.
- Nobody respects me.
- Nobody appreciates me.

Please notice that I'm asking you to question whether you should *believe* stressful thoughts or not. I'm not saying that you shouldn't *have* stressful thoughts. Since brains are naturally negative, it would be unreasonable to expect yourself to stop having stressful or judgmental thoughts. All I'm inviting you to do, initially, is to *notice* that you have numerous stressful thoughts and to not automatically believe them or act based on them.

Because stressful thoughts are common, many of us have grown accustomed to living with them. Perhaps, we even think that though they're irritating, the thoughts are probably harmless. I wish that was true. Long-standing negative thoughts about yourself such as, "I don't know what to do" or about other people such as, "He's clueless; he's not going to work out" might seem inconsequential. However, they could be destroying confidence in yourself and others. Negative thoughts erode confidence, because you begin to believe them. And, when you believe a thought, you act as if it's true.

So, instead of letting unpleasant thoughts sit around and gather dust, it's important to do something proactive with them. The best way that I've found to clean up negative thoughts is to investigate them. Investigating a stressful thought is like picking up an old coat in your closet and analyzing it with questions like: How long have I had this? How does it look on me? How do I feel and act when I wear it? How would I feel and act without it in my wardrobe? What could I get to replace it?

INVESTIGATING YOUR THOUGHTS

The most helpful tool I've found for investigating negative thoughts is **The Work©**, an inquiry process developed by Byron Katie (Byron Katie 2003, 2006, 2008). The Work© is a simple yet powerful inquiry process that teaches you to identify and question thoughts that cause stress. It's a way to understand what's upsetting you and to address problems with clarity in order to reduce suffering. You can read more about Byron Katie and The Work© at thework.com. (You can listen to a radio interview I did with her at goodradioshows.org; click on Peace Talks Episodes, then click on 2007).

Before you read any further, take ten minutes now to complete the **JUDGE YOUR NEIGHBOR WORKSHEET Work Out Box**. This exercise uses a powerful tool that Katie developed for doing The Work©: the Judge-Your-Neighbor Worksheet (© 2011 Byron Katie Inc.) Completing a Judge-Your-Neighbor Worksheet© will help you better understand how I used The Work© to help Karen regain her confidence to help Mark regain his confidence to help his assistant regain her confidence.

WORK OUT BOX

| USING THE JUDGE-YOUR-NEIGHBOR WORKSHEET©

To understand how The Work© helps you identify and investigate negative thoughts to feel more relaxed and confident, make a copy of the Judge-Your-Neighbor Worksheet© on the next page or have paper available for writing your answers to the questions. You can also access and print copies of it from Katie's website at http://www.thework.com/downloads/JudgeYourNeighbor.pdf.

1. With your eyes open or closed, feel your breath for one minute and get into a calm state.

2. Think of a person at work whom you haven't fully forgiven. The first time you do this Work Out, pick someone who you are mildly to moderately upset with as opposed to someone with whom you are extremely irritated.

3. Follow the instructions at the top of the Judge-Your-Neighbor Worksheet©, and fill in the blanks for the six statements.

4. For each of your six statements, ask yourself the four questions and complete the Turnarounds on the bottom of the Worksheet.

5. When you finish, feel your breath for another minute to relax and calm yourself.

6. Write in your journal what you noticed during this exercise.

THE WORK
of Byron Katie™

Judge-Your-Neighbor Worksheet

Judge your neighbor • Write it down • Ask four questions • Turn it around

Think of a recurring stressful situation, a situation that is reliably stressful even though it may have happened only once and recurs only in your mind. Before answering each of the questions below, allow yourself to mentally revisit the time and place of the stressful occurrence. Don't be polite, kind, or wise.

1. In this situation, time, and location, who angers, confuses, or disappoints you, and why?

   I am _____ with _____ because _____.
         emotion   *name*

   Example: I am angry with Paul because he argues with everything I say.

2. In this situation, how do you want them to change? What do you want them to do?

   I want _____ to _____
         name

   Example: I want Paul to see that he is wrong. I want him to apologize.

3. In this situation, what advice would you offer to **them**?

   _____ should/shouldn't _____
       name

   Example: Paul should take better care of himself. He shouldn't argue with me. He should stop lying. He should see that I am only trying to help him.

4. In order for *you* to be happy in this situation, what do you need them to think, say, feel, or do?

   I need _____ to _____
         name

   Example: I need Paul to hear me. I need Paul to respect me.

5. What do you think of them in this situation? Make a list.

   _____ is _____
       name

   Example: Paul is unfair, arrogant, loud, dishonest, way out of line, and unconscious.

6. What is it in or about this situation that you don't ever want to experience again?

   I don't ever want _____

   Example: I don't ever want to feel unappreciated by Paul again. I don't ever want to see him smoking and ruining his health again.

The Four Questions

Example: Paul doesn't listen to me.

1. Is it true?
2. Can you absolutely know that it's true?
3. How do you react, what happens, when you believe that thought?
4. Who would you be without the thought?

Turn the thought around

  a) to the self. (*I don't listen to me.*)
  b) to the other. (*I don't listen to Paul.*)
  c) to the opposite. (*Paul does listen to me.*)

And find three genuine, specific examples of how each turnaround is true for you in this situation.

For more information on how to do The Work, visit www.thework.com

Before our next call, Karen emailed the statements from her Judge-Your-Neighbor Worksheet© to me. She had written a worksheet about Mark:

1. I am angry at Mark because he isn't trying hard enough to hold Dana accountable.

2. I want Mark to tell Dana to stop crying about the payroll.

3. Mark should set stronger boundaries with Dana about her crying.

4. I need Mark to show me he is an effective leader.

5. Mark is afraid, a pushover, and unable to go outside his comfort zone as a leader.

6. I don't ever want to experience Mark complaining about Dana's crying again.

After we did The Work© on these beliefs, Karen realized that her own fear and delay about holding Mark accountable was setting a poor example for him. By the end of our call, she was not only ready to be more assertive with him, she was excited to teach him The Work© and help him develop a plan for addressing Dana's behavior. When we talked two weeks later, Karen reported the following story about Mark and Dana.

CASE STUDY: "THINGS ARE FALLING APART."

Mark ran the cardiac pharmaceutical laboratory in Karen's division. His assistant, Dana, was highly competent, but eager to retire in a year. Even though she had been nervous processing the division's payroll, Dana had asked her co-worker, Lance, for help with it when she needed it. When Lance moved to another department and Dana had some serious medical problems, the payroll issues that used to be mildly confusing became overwhelming. Though Dana began making more mistakes on payroll, she wouldn't ask anyone for help.

In the past when Mark tried to address her payroll errors, Dana would say she felt guilty and apologize profusely. When Mark asked her why she wouldn't ask for help from Carol in the Payroll Department, Dana would get angry, and say that Mark was the boss and should know the answers to her payroll questions. Mark replied that he was a lab manager who wasn't responsible for knowing about payroll, and that payroll was Dana's job. When Mark spoke firmly like that, Dana would cry. When Dana cried, Mark lost his confidence to be direct, switched to offering emotional support, and ended the meeting. Even though Mark continued to use this reactive leadership pattern of moving back and forth between aggressive and passive for months, Dana still refused to ask Carol for help.

After she learned The Work©, Karen told Mark that she wanted to help him address Dana's crying in a different way. As Mark described his latest interactions with Dana to Karen, he became very tense and said, "Things are falling apart." Karen noted to herself that instead of accurately *describing what was happening* with his team, Mark's statement *revealed his lack of confidence* with the situation.

Karen described The Work© to Mark and asked if he would like to try using it on his beliefs about Dana. When he agreed, Karen asked Mark to write his negative thought on paper. Then, she asked him questions from the Judge-Your-Neighbor Worksheet©.

KAREN: Is it true that things are falling apart?

MARK: Not completely. There are a lot of good things happening in the office, too. And, other than payroll, Dana's work is excellent.

KAREN: How do you react when you believe the thought, "Things are falling apart"?

MARK: I feel burdened and tense. I can't see the progress in my lab or in Dana. I'm also having some personal challenges that are draining my energy and making me feel overwhelmed at work.

KAREN: Who would you be without the thought, "Things are falling apart"?

MARK: I'd be calm. I'd be a better leader for Dana and help her find solutions to the crying and to learning payroll.

KAREN: What's a turnaround of the belief, "Things are falling apart"?

MARK: Things aren't falling apart. That's true, too.

KAREN: What are three reasons that the turnaround, "Things aren't falling apart" is true?

MARK: Dana is an excellent employee. She's very smart. And, she's interested in learning new tools. If I shared The Work© with her, I think it could really help her with the crying and with getting payroll done.

With Karen's help, Mark made a plan. He outlined how he would tell Dana that he wanted to be supportive while also setting clear expectations for her completing the payroll. Mark recognized that his leadership style tended to offer more support than structure; he wanted to change that pattern in his next conversation with Dana. As he and Karen continued to talk, Mark *noticed* that the thought "Things are falling apart" had disappeared. He could see how that belief had eroded his confidence to be firm. With his self-assurance back, he was ready to talk with Dana.

MARK AND DANA'S CONVERSATION

A few days later, Mark reported back to Karen that his conversation with Dana went well. He said that she didn't cry right away which was good, though she was uncomfortable. Then, as she began complaining about her job, she started to cry. He stayed calm, because he had a plan for what to do next. Here's how he described the conversation with Dana.

> MARK (feeling his Feet & Seat): Dana, you look upset. How would you feel about me asking you a few questions about what you're experiencing right now?
>
> DANA (sobbing quietly): Okay.
>
> MARK: What thoughts are you having right now as you're crying?
>
> DANA: I'm thinking, "I'm inadequate to do the payroll. Everyone knows what I did wrong, and they think I'm dumb."
>
> MARK: Dana, your thought, "I'm inadequate to do the payroll," is that true?
>
> DANA: What do you mean?
>
> MARK: Can you absolutely know that the thought, "I'm inadequate to do the payroll" is a factually true statement?

DANA: No. I guess I'm not completely inadequate. I get the basics. It's the special cases that I haven't figured out.

MARK: How do you react when you think the thought, "I'm inadequate to do the payroll"?

DANA: I feel anxious and embarrassed. Then, I stop trying and give up which makes me feel guilty and inadequate.

MARK: Who would you be without the thought, "I'm inadequate to do the payroll"?

DANA: I guess I'd be more relaxed and try to figure out the special cases.

They talked a little bit about the amygdala and how her stressful thoughts made her feel upset. Suddenly, Dana commented that talking about her feelings had calmed her down. She was no longer crying.

As they continued discussing her tasks, Dana made some neutral comments like, "This isn't a stressful job" and "Learning payroll isn't that different than solving any other problem I have at work." Mark encouraged her to write down the first belief, and post it over her desk. He said that seeing the neutral thought might remind her brain to look for examples of how her job isn't stressful.

Once Dana calmed down, Mark asked **Open-Ended Questions** (See **Chapter 6** on the Influence Tools) to help her identify anxiety triggers while working on payroll. They learned that not only did Dana always hate numbers, but Lance – the co-worker who trained her on payroll, unfortunately, told her to never ask the Payroll Department for help. Lance said it would show that she made mistakes.

DANA'S PAYROLL PLAN

Using The Work© and other communication tools, Mark skillfully helped Dana untangle how her thoughts, body sensations, and emotions lead to payroll errors, crying, and the inability to ask for help. However, they weren't finished.

Dana wanted a plan for approaching payroll in a new way. First, instead of telling herself, as she had in the past, that she should "get through payroll error-free," Dana committed to work through the payroll and leave the "error free" part out. Second, she would calm herself while doing the payroll by using the **Feet & Seat** MP. Third, as soon as she checked her work, Dana would call Carol in the Payroll Department and say, "I've just sent the payroll. Can you tell me if any errors come up and walk me through the process to fix them?"

When Mark reported all of this good news to Karen, she encouraged him to acknowledge Dana's progress in some way, for example, writing her a personal note or affirming her in their next one-on-one meeting. The postscript to this case is that Dana became skilled at running payroll, and she never cried again in her meetings with Mark.

EXPLORATION STEPS AND TOOLS

To help you use the Exploration process, I created three simple steps and collected some helpful tools. The three steps – **Listen - Inquire Affirm** – develop the Exploration process that over time cultivates a mindset of Confidence. The Explorations Tools are three practices that you can use in silent or active settings. Remember that the steps and tools build on the confident foundation that you're noticing and building based on the Confident Leader Assessment (themindtolead.com).

THE EXPLORATION STEPS: LISTEN - INQUIRE - AFFIRM

The Leadership Attunement Model (Figure 5.1) shows how to use the Exploration Steps – **Listen - Inquire - Affirm** – in two contexts: with "Self" and "Other." Apply the Exploration Steps to attune with yourself or with the other person. These options include:

- Be confident while solo
- Be confident with the other person
- Help the other person be confident

Mark's case study is a good example of how to use The Work© to increase confidence in yourself and others.

FIGURE 5.1 LEADERSHIP ATTUNEMENT MODEL: CONFIDENT LEADER

MINDSET	CONFIDENT
PROCESS	Exploration
STEPS SELF	• **LISTEN** to your thoughts about yourself and the other person. • **INQUIRE** using The Work©. • **AFFIRM** your action plan and three things that are working well.
OTHER	• **LISTEN** to the other person's thoughts about the situation/issue. • **INQUIRE** using The Work©. • **AFFIRM** the action plan and three things that are working well.
TOOLS	• Judge-Your-Neighbor Worksheet© at thework.com • Compassion Practice

BE CONFIDENT WHILE SOLO

In the safety briefing before a plane takes off, the flight attendant explains that if the cabin pressure changes, you should put your mask on first before trying to help someone else with theirs. It works the same way with the Exploration Steps.

Put your mask on first – be confident before you go into a conversation – so that you can be self-assured during the conversation regardless of what happens. When you're confident going into a conversation, you'll be a better listener, more curious, and a superior problem-solving partner even if the other person is resisting you.

Imagine if Mark hadn't *listened* to and *inquired* into his own negative thoughts before talking with Dana, or if he hadn't *affirmed* his action plan for their conversation. If he hadn't stated aloud to himself and Karen, "Things are falling apart," it's likely that this stressful thought could have surfaced in his mind – as it had in the past – when Dana started crying. If Mark was thinking that Dana, his department, and his leadership style were falling apart, how effective would he be at helping her figure out why she was upset?

In the first Exploration step, Mark *listened* to his unpleasant thoughts as he said them to Karen and wrote them on a piece of paper. Writing his thoughts helped him see them more objectively.

In the second Exploration step with Karen's help, Mark used The Work© to *inquire* about what was true and the impact of his stressful thoughts on his leadership behavior with Dana. In the third step, Mark *affirmed t*he reality of the situation. Things weren't falling apart; in fact, most of Dana's performance was excellent. He also *affirmed* a plan both for keeping the conversation going even if Dana began crying and for holding her accountable to learn payroll.

BE CONFIDENT WITH THE OTHER PERSON

During their conversation when Karen taught The Work© to Mark, she warned him that negative thoughts might resurface in his mind if Dana started crying. Karen coached Mark on how to stay confident even if the crying brought up Mark's old thoughts which might tempt him to fall back into old behavior patterns.

KAREN: Mark, can you play a video of yourself talking with Dana, and then see her starting to cry?

MARK: Yep, I can see that easily.

KAREN: What thoughts are coming up for you as she cries?

MARK: Let's see, "I made her cry," "I don't know what to do now," and "I should stop the conversation."

KAREN: Good job identifying your stressful thoughts. What's your interest level in doing The Work© on your own on each of those beliefs before you talk with her?

MARK: If it doesn't take much time, I can see that would be valuable. I can use the forms you gave me, right?

KAREN: Yes, and let me know if you have any questions about how to do it on your own. It only takes me about five minutes per stressful thought. I think that doing The Work© on those three thoughts before your conversation with Dana could help your confidence. What will you do if she starts crying and those stressful thoughts come up anyway?

MARK: I don't know. What do you suggest?

KAREN: When my coach, Suzanne, was helping me plan for this conversation with you, she taught me how to do a mini-version of The Work© during a conversation.

MARK: What do you mean?

KAREN: Frankly, Mark, I was nervous to talk with you about Dana. I had my own limiting beliefs like, "Mark isn't trying hard enough to hold Dana accountable."

MARK (laughing): I guess you turned that around to you weren't trying hard enough to hold me accountable.

KAREN (smiling): Yes, you're right. And, that ah-ha helped me realize that I needed to offer you both more structure and support. That's why we're talking today. Suzanne suggested that I *listen* in my mind to see if that thought or other stressful thoughts came up during our conversation today. If one did, then I could silently and quickly *inquire* in my mind, "Is it true?" She said that simply asking the first question might help me regain my confidence. I'll be honest, I was nervous when you and I first started talking about The Work© today. You seemed a bit resistant, and I caught myself thinking, "He doesn't want to try this" and "He thinks this is crazy." After I caught each thought, and asked, "Is it true?," I *affirmed* that I was jumping to conclusions and needed to give you more time to talk about it. After about five more minutes of discussion, you were ready to try The Work©, and it seemed to go well for you.

MARK: That's interesting. I had no idea you were unsure at any point in our conversation today. You seemed relaxed, Karen. Actually, you spoke more confidently about your expectations of me with Dana than you ever have before. Hmm. I get it. So, I need to be vigilant during my conversation with Dana. What were the steps? **Listen, inquire,** and **affirm**?

KAREN: Yes, that's it, Mark. And, thanks for acknowledging how I came across today. Because I caught my negative thoughts pretty quickly, they didn't seem to lower my confidence. I'm happy that you're willing to try The Work© before and during your conversation with Dana.

HELP THE OTHER BE CONFIDENT

When a mindful leader encounters resistance from a person or group, their opposition is often due to a lack of confidence. In other words, sometimes people complain because they feel insecure about taking the next step. In situations like that, it might be appropriate to use questions from The Work© to help people regain confidence. As a confident leader, Mark was able to effectively guide Dana through the Exploration Steps.

In the first step, Mark *listened* carefully to Dana's stressful thoughts and judgments about her job, processing the payroll, and even her belief that Mark should know how to do the payroll. Because he was confident, Mark wasn't thrown off by that comment. He verbally gave the responsibility back to her, so that Dana could own her discomfort about her job.

In the second step, Mark *inquired* about Dana's discomfort. When he used The Work©, it helped her see that the payroll challenges weren't any harder than other issues she'd successfully resolved in her career. And, talking about her feelings and her capabilities calmed Dana down.

In the third step, Mark helped Dana *affirm* both the reality of her present situation – "This is not a stressful job" – as well as a plan for a better future. Once Dana got to a more neutral, confident mind state, Mark helped her plan how to calmly process the payroll and ask for help with errors.

When some leaders first encounter The Work©, they're concerned that the questions sound like therapy. To clarify, therapy is about the past; The Work© is about investigating the present. *Notice* that Mark didn't ask Dana, "How did your parents treat

MIND TRICK BOX

| THE NEUROSCIENCE OF COMPASSION

Research shows that compassion practice is good for your brain and your ability to relate to people. Antoine Lutz at the University of Wisconsin did studies with two different groups of colleagues that show the impact of compassion practice on the brain. In the studies, compassion was defined as an "unrestricted readiness and availability to help living beings" (Lutz et al. 2004, 16369). Each study compared two groups: (1) long-term meditation practitioners who had from 10,000 to 50,000 hours of meditation experience (yes, they missed a lot of television) and (2) novices from the university community who had no meditation experience but an interest in learning to meditate.

A week before data collection, the novices were given meditation instructions and asked to practice daily for 20 to 60 minutes. Then, researchers collected data on all of the subjects' brains during compassion meditation as well as during a neutral mental state.

In **Chapter 4**, I described how results from the first study showed that compassion meditation was associated with gamma wave oscillations that were significantly higher for the experienced practitioners than for the novices (Lutz et al. 2004, 16371). A gamma wave is a pattern of brain waves produced when masses of neurons emit electrical signals at the rate of around 25-42 times a second (Hertz or Hz), but can often be over 70 Hz. Gamma waves are associated with higher mental activities like perception and insight as well as with increased levels of compassion and happiness. Gamma waves can also serve as a binding mechanism between all parts of the brain and can help improve memory and perception. All of these qualities can be helpful for leaders.

In the second study, Lutz and colleagues were curious about the impact of compassion meditation on emotional reaction (Lutz et al. 2008, 1). Since one of the long-term goals of compassion training is to reduce a person's egocentric reactions and increase his spontaneous concern for others, the researchers wanted to see if that really happened in long-term meditators. While subjects were in both meditative and neutral states, researchers played three different sounds: negative (such as a distressed woman), positive (such as a baby laughing), and neutral (such as background noise in a restaurant). They ran functional MRI scans to measure the emotional reactions to the different sounds (Lutz et al. 2008, 2).

Lutz and colleagues expected three things: a stronger empathic response to the negative sounds than the positive or neutral sounds, a stronger response during meditation than at rest, and a stronger response in the experienced meditators than the novices. All three of those responses happened in the subjects' brains (Lutz et al. 2008, 2). These results suggest that developing a compassionate mind state can improve a person's ability to empathetically respond to social stimuli.

The researchers think that while expert meditators are in a compassionate state, they might be more able to detect interpersonal cues such as another person's discomfort or suffering (Lutz et al. 2008, 6). This, too, could be an important skill for leaders to have.

For a radio interview I did with one of the researchers in these studies, Dr. Richard Davidson, as well as with Dr. Dan Siegel, go to goodradioshows.org, and click on Peace Talk Episodes in 2008.

you?" or "What made you cry as a child?" Questions about Dana's personal life would have been inappropriate. Instead, Mark asked questions about the present moment like, "How do you react when you think that thought?"

When a leader is hesitant to use The Work© to help someone build confidence, I recommend that he begin by simply asking the other person the first question, "Is that true?" Over time, when he sees that this one question often reduces the negative impact of complaints and self-defeating comments, he is more likely to use all of the questions.

EXPLORATION TOOLS

Other than attuning your **Reporter** to *listen* for negative thoughts and using The Work© to *inquire* about their validity and impact, there's only one other Exploration tool that helps build confidence. One of the reasons that people lack confidence in the workplace is because of a tendency to judge oneself as inferior or superior to others. Compassion Practice levels the playing field and helps us remember that life is challenging for everyone.

COMPASSION PRACTICE

Compassion is empathy for a person's suffering, and often includes a desire to help. This is a theory on my part: A mindful leader is more likely to feel and express compassion for his employees, colleagues, and boss when he feels confident. The confident leaders I know don't feel a need to protect themselves or hoard power. When appropriate, they let their guard down and show that they care about people at work.

Compassion practice is different than the Mindfulness Practices. The MPs develop a cool awareness and acceptance of the way things are. That approach is good, because sometimes a leader benefits by simply observing and being with whatever success or difficulty is happening in the present moment. Compassion practice, on the other hand, is warm and generative. A mindful leader uses it to comfort and build confidence in himself or in others during a challenging time. It's good to develop both types of practice and to be able to flex back and forth between them throughout your workday.

WORK OUT BOX
| COMPASSION PRACTICE

1. Get in a comfortable position sitting or lying down. Close your eyes, and move your awareness into the center of your chest. As you inhale and exhale deeply three times, feel the movement of your breath relaxing your chest. Then, let go of the deep breathing, and allow your breath to find its own rhythm. Feel the breath move in and out of your chest for a minute or two.

2. Keep your awareness on your chest. Think of a person. Create a positive image of the person, and place the image in your chest or emotional heart center. If that feels uncomfortable, place the image outside your body in front of your chest. See an image that naturally evokes your compassion for that person.

3. With the image inside or outside your chest, slowly and silently say your phrases either in your mind or aloud. Say a phrase about every three to five seconds; develop a pace that's comfortable. You don't need to rush the phrases. However, don't allow too much time in between phrases, or there's a tendency for your mind to wander to something else. The image may come and go. When you *notice* that it's gone, gently recall it.

4. If you do relatively well focusing your awareness on the image and phrases, you can add a kinesthetic aspect to this practice. As you continue to practice, generate a felt sense of what you are wishing for. What does it feel like in your body to be happy? To be safe? Shift your image a bit to see your selected person experiencing those sensations, too.

Adding this kinesthetic piece is easier to do when you're using just one phrase, because you maintain the same sensation throughout your practice period. If you're using a series of three or four phrases, it's a bit more challenging to shift body sensations with each phrase, for example from safe to happy to healthy to ease. However, it can be done. Take your time, and enjoy the felt sense of each of those wonderful qualities.

5. Write in your journal what you noticed during this exercise.

PREPARING FOR COMPASSION

In compassion practice, you consciously create experiences in the physical, mental, and emotional realms in order to experience caring feelings. While you might be a naturally caring person even with people at work, compassion practice lets you be more intentional about generating empathy for yourself and others. Here are some preparatory steps to take before doing the practice in the **COMPASSION PRACTICE Work Out Box**.

First, select a person or group as your object of compassion. It could be yourself, an employee, your boss, your team, the entire organization, or an even larger group like all of the people in your state, country, or the world. Next, identify up to four short sentences or phrases that you want to send to your selected person(s). Think about what the person needs most right now. For example, if you need to deliver some challenging feedback to a direct report, you might use the phrase for him, "May you be free from worry." If you want to prepare yourself for the conversation, a phrase for yourself might be, "May I be kind."

Select phrases that are easy to remember and have a strong meaning for you. Keep the ideas simple and the phrases short, 12 words or less.

Call to mind positive thoughts, feelings, and images about your selected person that will generate empathy. At the beginning of each practice period, think about times in the past when the person did something that reflected his best qualities. In your mind, see the person portraying these qualities such as kindness, generosity, humor, or courage. If you selected yourself as the compassion recipient, call to mind what's good about you.

After you select a person, the phrases, and supportive evidence of what makes the person likeable, spend about ten minutes doing Compassion Practice.

In summary, you can increase your confidence as a mindful leader. Train your mind to *listen* for your negative thoughts, write them on paper, *inquire* as to the validity of the thoughts using The Work©, and then *affirm* what is true, what is working well, and what action steps you want to take. Now that you have skills for developing a calm, confident leadership style, let's look at how to use power appropriately.

CONCEPTS

- Negative thoughts erode leader confidence. Instead of believing your stressful thoughts, be curious. Investigate whether your thoughts are true and the impact they have on your attitude and behavior.

- The Exploration Steps – **LISTEN - INQUIRE - AFFIRM** – help you identify and examine your negative thoughts, and then create an action plan based on the reality of the situation.

- The Work©, an inquiry process developed by Byron Katie (thework.com), may help you let go of negative thinking patterns, so that you feel and act with confidence.

- As you begin to feel safer and more confident as a mindful leader, use compassion practice to generate feelings of kindness for yourself and others.

CHAPTER 6

MINDSET 3:
INFLUENCE TRAINING FOR POWERFUL LEADERS

On our next call, Karen was excited about Mark's success.

KAREN: It's amazing, Suzanne. Mark has had no more problems
with Dana. She hasn't cried anymore, and last week's payroll
was error-free. Mark is so relieved, and the whole experience has
boosted his confidence to be more direct with all of his employees.

SUZANNE: That's great. And, how's your confidence these days?

KAREN: Much better. Remember when I asked you to talk with
Mark, because I felt clueless about what to do next? When you
said, "No, I want to help you help Mark," I have to admit I was a
bit angry with you, Suzanne. I thought I hired you to be my go-to
fix-it gal. Once I realized that your job is to encourage me through
the hard stuff, rather than to do the hard stuff for me, and you gave
me The Work© to deal with my insecurity about holding Mark
accountable, wow, I got it! And, because I had walked through the
fire in making myself talk with him, it was easy to expect the same
from him. I knew he could get through this challenging situation
with Dana. It was a powerful learning experience for me. I feel like
I can handle anything now. Thank you so much.

SUZANNE: You're welcome. Your social intelligence is thriving.
And, even though you can't know what's around the corner, you're
confident that you have the tools to handle whatever's next. How
would you describe your experience of confidence in the four

realms?

KAREN: Physically, I have more energy. Even at the end of a super busy day, there's less fatigue or jangliness. Maybe that's because I gave up my afternoon coffee! Mentally, there's less thinking about the future. Well, that's not true, because I'm actually thinking more about plans for the future. It's that there's less worrying about what's coming next or how I'll defend something, particularly with my boss. Emotionally, I feel, what would the word be? Unruffled, more poised. And, behaviorally, I'm getting more done. Mindfulness practice helps me concentrate better, so I get tasks done a bit faster, even the ones I dread. My conversations with most people are shorter than before, because I'm more self-assured and direct. However, I'm still experiencing some problems with a couple managers. At some point, I'd like your help dealing with resistance, particularly from people who are older, smarter, and more experienced than I am. Anyway, overall, I've seen big improvements.

SUZANNE: Outstanding. What would you like to talk about today?

KAREN: Because these tools have helped me so much, I want to share them with my management team. I know you said that we could do an in-person coaching conversation when I'm in DC in a few months. I was wondering if, instead, we could bring you to San Francisco this month to meet with my team.

SUZANNE: I'd love to come out and work with your team, Karen. Thanks very much for the invitation.

Karen and I talked about some options for how to use my time. She decided that she wanted the first day to be shadow coaching where I would spend the day watching her in action then we'd do coaching on my observations. The second day would be an offsite leadership retreat with her and her eight managers including Janice, Bob, and Mark who I already knew a little about. On the last day, I would do an individual coaching session with each of the managers.

To prepare for the management team retreat, I conducted confidential phone interviews with a random sample of four managers. We talked about their successes and challenges. I asked what was working well in their own teams and on the management team as well as where they wanted to see improvements. The interview results showed:

- Employees are loyal to the company and most have a good attitude. However, there are pockets of problems with absenteeism and poor performance.

- The lab teams meet their goals and have good productivity, though there are instances of unresolved conflict and a desire for meetings to be more efficient.

- Management team relations are fair. They do a good job, sharing employees when needed, however a few managers have conflicting personality styles and others don't always follow company policies and procedures.

- Team leadership by Karen is good. They see her as a visionary leader and feel that she does a good job securing resources from her boss, Gary. However, they want to see her push back on what they feel are his unrealistic expectations for growing the business.

- Internal customers are very satisfied, because the labs develop and test new drugs on time and often under budget. The labs are well-respected in the industry for exceeding Food and Drug Administration regulations. This makes it easy for the marketing division to promote their pharmaceuticals to doctors and hospitals.

Based on this input, I suggested to Karen that I facilitate my Powerful Leader retreat for the offsite. This retreat teaches seven communication tools for handling resistance and conflict. It also includes a simple style assessment and covers how to manage resistance from each of the four style types. This curriculum could help the managers be more effective in handling performance issues and conflict on their own teams as well as with each other. Karen liked the idea to focus on power, resistance, and styles. I asked her to send the link to my Powerful Leader Assessment to her management team and have them complete it before the retreat (themindtolead.com).

Karen scheduled the shadow coaching for my first day so that I could observe her in a variety of situations with, for example, a few of her managers, her boss, and her entire management team. She was excited. And, I was looking forward to the chance to support Karen and her team.

CASE STUDY: "HOW YOU TALK WITH TEAM MEMBERS NEEDS TO CHANGE."

On the first morning, I met Karen in her office at 7:30.

> KAREN: I thought we'd start the day off with a bang. We're going to meet with Randall, the manager of the genetics diagnostics lab, and one of his project teams. I don't usually attend lab meetings. However, I'm having some problems with Randall and wanted you to see him in action.

> SUZANNE: How do you think he'll respond with me in the room?

> KAREN: Nothing fazes this guy. I told him last week that you and I would be sitting in. He shrugged his shoulders, and changed the subject. Randall is all about facts. I don't think people issues register on his Richter scale. That's why I need your help. Several of his employees have complained to me that he makes harsh comments particularly about young people on the team. I'm having trouble discussing this behavioral issue with him. We better get started, Suzanne. It'll take us awhile to get to the conference room on the 3rd floor.

On the elevator, Karen filled me in on Randall. About a year ago, he approached her at a conference. He was a 58-year-old scientist working at the Cleveland Clinic and internationally known for his genetics research. He asked Karen about a position on her management team, because he wanted to move back to the Bay area to be near his aging parents. Karen was excited. Unfortunately, in her haste to bring him on board, she didn't take the time to research his interpersonal skills or teaming experience.

> KAREN: He interrupts people all the time. And, he puts people down by saying things like, "That's not how we did it at Stanford. It's an outdated approach and won't work." I've tried several times to point out that this type of language is de-motivating. Basically, he just blows me off, too.

> SUZANNE: How can I help you today?

KAREN: I told him that you and I were observing some team meetings so that you could get a sense of the division's work. I'm not
planning on saying anything in the meeting. I'd like you to watch
Randall and the team dynamics. Let's talk afterwards about how I
can address his behavior.

The meeting was just starting as Karen and I took seats outside of the group against
the wall. As the meeting progressed, Randall was clearly in control doing most of the
talking and cutting people off even after asking the group for input. After each team
member gave a brief update on his or her work, Randall made a few comments usually
pointing out something the report lacked or expressing a concern about how closely
the individual was following lab protocol.

With about 10 minutes left before the end of the meeting, Brittany, the team lead on
a new cancer diagnostic, mentioned her concern about meeting an upcoming deadline
for a deliverable.

BRITTANY: Randall, I could use some help running the final tests.
I talked with Ryan about this, and he said he could contribute 15
hours next week to help. Is that okay with you?

As Ryan nodded his head in agreement, Randall's eyes widened and his head
pulled back.

RANDALL: I don't want that kid on this project. It's too important.
Who else could help?

Ryan's head dropped, and he stared at the table. The room was silent. I felt an ache
in my chest and saw Karen's hands clench her pen. I wondered if she would speak up
or not.

After a few moments, Randall continued.

RANDALL: Beth and John, I want each of you to give Brittany ten
hours next week. Let me know if that's a problem. That's it everyone. Same time next week.

Randall nodded at Karen and I as he walked out the door.

A few team members walked over to say hello to Karen and I. Though no one
mentioned Randall's comment, tension was still hanging in the room.

Karen and I had some time to talk in her office before our next meeting.

KAREN: That was worse than usual. I felt so tense and angry, and Ryan, I felt so horrible for him. I need to address this with Randall immediately. (Lifting her phone receiver and calling her assistant) Tommy, tell Randall to be in my office in 30 minutes.

SUZANNE: What do you most want from our conversation, Karen?

KAREN: Let's talk through this. Then I'll meet with Randall while you observe Bob's team meeting. How do I communicate firmly that his behavior is unacceptable while also figuring out the root of it? I know that asking, "Why in the world did you do that?" won't get him anywhere. Yet, I want to help him shine a light on this behavior pattern, so that he understands it.

SUZANNE: What do you think the behavior is about?

KAREN: I have no idea.

SUZANNE: I'm guessing that you're upset and embarrassed about the meeting. Am I right?

KAREN: Yes, I'm mortified that the first thing you saw is one of my managers totally out of control. And, I'm angry at myself. I feel incompetent as a leader. Crap, I feel so angry. Let me take a few minutes to calm down and check in with myself.

We sat in silence while Karen took a few deep breaths with long exhales. We had about 20 minutes before her meeting with Randall. It was just enough time to review the Influence Steps and a few tools.

THE INFLUENCE STEPS AND TOOLS

The Influence Steps – **Speak - Observe - Focus** – develop the Influence process that over time cultivates a mindset of power. The Influence Tools are seven skills to help you manage your direct reports as well as your boss and colleagues. The steps and tools build on the power foundation that you can develop and maintain by using the upgrades in the Powerful Leader Assessment (themindtolead.com).

THE INFLUENCE STEPS: SPEAK - OBSERVE - FOCUS

The Leadership Attunement Model (Figure 6.1) shows how to use the Influence Steps – **Speak - Observe - Focus** – in two contexts: with "Self" and "Other." To use power appropriately, apply the Influence Steps before and during interactions with others, and particularly in challenging situations. Later in this chapter, I'll explain how to use each of the Influence Tools during the steps. First, let's look at how to use the steps in two important ways:

- Use power appropriately to influence yourself
- Use power appropriately to influence others

FIGURE 6. 1 LEADERSHIP ATTUNEMENT MODEL: POWERFUL LEADER

MINDSET	POWER
PROCESS	Influence
STEPS	
SELF	• **SPEAK** my intention in a concise statement to myself. • **OBSERVE** my reaction. • **FOCUS** my mind on my expected outcome.
OTHER	• **SPEAK** my expectation in a concise statement to the other person. • **OBSERVE** the other person's reaction. • **FOCUS** the other person's mind on my expected outcome.
TOOLS	• Laser Message • Pause • Venting • Facts & Feelings • Open-Ended Questions • BEER • Flexing Your Style

USE POWER APPROPRIATELY TO INFLUENCE YOURSELF

After Karen finished a few minutes of reflection, she opened her eyes.

KAREN: When I'm tense and embarrassed and angry, I'm not leading. I'm immobilized and caught up in my own feelings rather than
focused on how to resolve the situation. I want to help Randall
understand and improve his behavior.

SUZANNE: You just completed the first Influence step by *speaking*
your intention in a concise statement to yourself. The second step is
to *observe* your reaction to that intention. What's your reaction?

KAREN: I feel calmer and stronger, even excited. It's funny, because I can't find any judgments of Randall, like "He's a jerk" or
"He's out of control." My mind is focused on my intention. I can
see myself talking with him in a composed, firm way.

SUZANNE: Nice work covering the **THREE INFLUENCE STEPS
WITH YOURSELF** (See **Work Out Box**). Your posture looks confident and relaxed. Keep playing the video. What laser statement are
you saying to Randall to summarize your expectation?

KAREN (pausing to reflect): How you talk with team members
needs to change.

I asked Karen to write the laser statement on paper. When her expectation is clear,
it's less likely that she'll be pulled off course by distracting thoughts or physical discomfort. This develops internal influence. Then when she *speaks* with Randall, if he is
resistant, she can simply *observe* his resistance and *focus* the conversation back on her
expectation. This is external influence.

We brainstormed some possible reactions – positive, negative, and neutral – that
Randall might have to Karen's laser statement and what she would say and do in each
case. Her job, regardless of what he said or did, was to calmly manage the tone and
purpose of the conversation without dominating Randall. Karen understood how important it was – if she became frustrated – to not fall into Randall's style of command
and offend. We also talked about how she could flex between two communication
styles – Ask versus Tell – to influence Randall.

As we were finishing up, there was a knock on Karen's door. We exchanged smiles. I opened the door, and as Randall walked in, I walked out.

WORK OUT BOX

| THREE INFLUENCE STEPS FOR USING POWER WITH YOURSELF

1. *Speak* your intention in a concise statement to yourself. To create this statement, ask yourself, "If there were no limits on what I think is achievable, what do I want in this situation?" Listen to yourself. Write what you want in one sentence.

2. *Observe* your reaction. What signals does your **Reporter** pick up? What *sensations* and *thoughts* surface as you see your intention on paper? What *feelings* do you have – fear and irritation, or excitement and confidence? How do these signals impact your *actions*? Use the Mindfulness and Exploration Steps and Tools to regain calm, confidence.

3. *Focus* your mind on your intention. Brainstorm and write down possible action steps such as researching the issue, communicating with others, or developing an alliance. Organize the best action steps into a concise plan with a timeline. Play a video of yourself taking the action steps to achieve your goal. As you implement the plan, keep your **Reporter** tuned in for distracting sensations, thoughts, feelings, or actions. Expect distractions. It's normal for your mind to be pulled off task. Make a game out of catching the distractions as quickly as possible and then regaining focus on your intention.

USE POWER APPROPRIATELY TO INFLUENCE OTHERS

At the end of Bob's team meeting, I walked back to Karen's office. She was busy answering emails.

KAREN: Have a seat, Suzanne. I'm almost finished with these. It went well with Randall. He got it. He got it right away. Why didn't I try the calm, direct approach with him before?

SUZANNE: When a leader *focuses* her mind on a single message that she believes in, the other person often picks up that something has changed. Randall intuitively knew that fighting, running, or hiding would no longer work.

KAREN: I was glad that you asked me to script what I wanted to say even though I didn't know exactly how he would respond to any of it. I also liked that I had these two basic approaches – Tell and Ask – and the tools to choose from (Figure 6.2). I started out by stating my expectation – "How you talk with team members needs to change." As we guessed, he immediately expressed resistance. So, I acknowledged his concerns by using the Tell tool you gave me, **Facts & Feelings**, to reflect the situation and his emotions back to him. I was afraid he wouldn't like the reflective approach, however, it worked beautifully. Let me tell you how it went.

Then, Karen recounted the dialogue from their conversation.

FIGURE 6.2. TELL AND ASK INFLUENCE TOOLS

	LOW RESISTANCE	MODERATE RESISTANCE	HIGH RESISTANCE
TELL	Laser Message	Facts & Feelings	BEER
ASK	Pause	Vent Open-Ended Questions	Flexing Your Style

KAREN: Randall, thanks for coming in. I want to talk with you about your behavior in the team meeting.

RANDALL (irritated): What's the problem? My team is submitting all their deliverables early and on budget. Sometimes under budget, Karen.

KAREN: Yes, thank you. I appreciate how you exceed expectations with deliverable timelines and budgets. This is a different issue; it's related to your communication style, Randall. [Pause] How you talk with team members needs to change [Laser Message].

RANDALL: That's ridiculous.

KAREN: Sounds like you're angry [**Feeling**] about my expectation [**Fact**].

RANDALL: Of course, I'm angry. It's insulting. I'm a senior research scientist known around the world for over 37 patents, and you're telling me I'm not good enough to work here.

KAREN: You're nervous [**Feeling**] that I'm going to fire you [**Fact**]?

RANDALL: Isn't that what you're suggesting?

KAREN: Absolutely not. You're a very skilled researcher. I want to keep you here as long as possible. The issue is that how you talk with team members needs to change [**Laser Message**].

RANDALL: I don't know about anyone else in this company, but I've got work to do. I don't have time to hold people's hands and make them feel good.

KAREN: It's irritating [**Feeling**] to have to slow down and train others who aren't as technically skilled as you [**Fact**], isn't it?

RANDALL: It's maddening. It's been this way my entire career. I'm tired of it. Even at Stanford when I was a research assistant and later with my dissertation committee. I had to explain my formulas to professors. It made me so angry.

Karen stopped relating the dialogue for a minute to comment on what she had learned.

KAREN: As I *spoke* my expectation, I *observed* how upset Randall was. He was leaning forward and talking fast. As I reflected my guesses about the facts and feelings of his situation, I *noticed* that he was mad at the circumstances and not mad at me. This was a big Ah-Ha! I also *observed* that he was very engaged in our conversation. And, my guess about him feeling irritated with training people was right on. When I said that, he sat back in his chair and sighed. He looked like he felt heard. I wondered if I was the first person he'd ever discussed this long-standing problem with. I'm not exactly a brainiac, so I never had that kind of challenge before – of being so smart. The conversation helped me understand Randall's aggravation with being smarter and quicker than everyone.

Karen remembered what I had said about being prepared to switch her mode from Tell to Ask and that the most important quality for her to develop was curiosity. Her questions gave him time to vent and talk through his frustration. That was what he needed to recognize that it was time for him to change. When Karen could see that he was calming down a little bit, she shifted to asking Open-Ended Questions as a way to let him own the issue. Then, she could *observe* when it was time to *focus* on her expectation again. Here's more of their dialogue.

KAREN: What was the worst part about explaining formulas to your professors? **[Open-Ended Question]**

RANDALL: I had to go really slowly. I hated that. Those guys were making the big bucks, but they didn't understand half of what I was talking about.

KAREN: How did you respond when they asked questions? **[Open-Ended Question]**

RANDALL: I was polite. That was my upbringing, to respect people in authority, at least in public. When I talked with my friends about it later, though, I would trash the professors.

KAREN: Randall, when did you start, can I use your word "trashing," your co-workers? **[Open-Ended Question]**

RANDALL: Okay, okay, you nailed it, Karen. I started in graduate school. I made fun of my peers in the lab. I always finished assignments first. Then, I'd walk around looking over people's shoulders and reading their formulas. I'd laugh at them and make sarcastic comments. I guess it was pretty mean. I've been doing that, in one way or another, for 36 years.

KAREN: What are the benefits of trying a new approach? [**Open-Ended Question**]

RANDALL: Maybe my employees would trust me and look up to me for more than technical knowledge.

KAREN: That's possible. How might you feel differently without the sarcastic comments? [**Open-Ended Question**]

RANDALL: I guess I'd save time and focus on the task and project. I might be more relaxed. I don't think it will be easy for me to stop this habit. I just do it automatically. But, I have to admit that being mad at people is draining. It's not Ryan's fault that he's a kid and doesn't know every equation in my mind. He doesn't need to. All he needs to run a lab test is to follow one formula over and over again.

Karen paused her story, looked at me, and shook her head in disbelief.

KAREN: Suzanne, I'm still a bit stunned with what came out of his mouth. Randall admitted that his behavior was inappropriate, and that he was willing to do whatever it takes to change this life-long pattern of putting people down. Instead of laying down the law and *telling* Randall what to do, I *asked* a series of solution-oriented questions using the five **Reporter** words you gave me. The questions let Randall develop his own action plan that even accounted for backsliding.

SUZANNE: That's terrific. Did you ask any of the questions that you wrote during our planning conversation?

KAREN: I used three of them: "To whom on the team do you

want to apologize?," "What behaviors of yours would you like to see change in team meetings?," and "When should we check in to evaluate your progress?" I added these two:

• Where can you find resources to help you learn new communication skills?

• How do you plan to handle a setback when you say something harsh?

I acknowledged Karen's impressive use of the **THREE INFLUENCE STEPS FOR USING POWER WITH OTHERS** with Randall (See **Work Out Box**). She was brave, benevolent, and balanced.

WORK OUT BOX
| THREE INFLUENCE STEPS FOR USING POWER WITH OTHERS

1. *Speak* your expectation in a concise statement to the other person. Use an appropriate MP to keep your body calm and your mind focused while you're talking with her.

2. *Observe* the other person's reaction. Use your **Reporter** to pick up signals from her. When you get uncomfortable, loop back to the Mindfulness Steps; **Notice - Breathe - Allow** her reaction and your reaction to it. Take mental notes on the reaction pattern between the two of you. What are the obvious and subtle verbal and nonverbal cues that say whether the conversation is working or not? What do each of you do or not do that sets the other off? Which productive or unproductive patterns, if any, do you want to surface and discuss in the meeting? Which patterns do you want to disregard or possibly address in a future meeting?

3. *Focus* the other person's mind on your expected outcome. Use the Influence Tools to reduce her resistance to your expectation, so that she develops and commits to an action plan. You don't have to reduce her resistance to zero. Less than 20% resistance is usually good enough to reach an agreement that she will take the first steps toward meeting your expectation. End the conversation by scheduling a follow-up conversation or email for her to report her progress.

KAREN: Thanks, Suzanne. One of my primary goals for coaching with you was to learn how to have these hard conversations. I mistakenly thought that would mean having to get tough with people. Now I see that, instead, I need to get clear and firm and sort of, out of the way.

SUZANNE: What do you mean?

KAREN: This sounds cliché, but, what I mean is these hard conversations – they're not about me. All I need to do is handle my Me stuff *before* the conversation, so that I can *focus* on the You stuff *during* the conversation. It's not that I was invisible or absent with Randall. I felt very present with him. It's just that *his* experience – his physical, mental, emotional, and behavioral responses – not *mine*, were the focus of the conversation.

Karen described that really well. And, there might be times in conversations when the other person's resistance is so strong that it would be appropriate for a mindful leader to disclose her experience, too.

As we were finishing up, Karen wondered how Randall would come across at the retreat tomorrow. She said I would love the location that Tommy found – a mansion in the historic section of San Francisco. Elegant and spacious with amazing gardens. Everyone was excited about it.

THE POWERFUL LEADER RETREAT

I met Tommy at the retreat site at 7:00 the next morning. Karen was right about the location. The mansion was warm and stately, a perfect get-away-from-the-office refreshing environment for the mind and body. Our meeting room had an entire wall of floor-to-ceiling windows that looked out on the bay. There were three long, white-linen covered tables in a U-shape facing the screen with handouts, pens, and chocolates perfectly arranged at each of the nine seats. Along the back wall, a lavish breakfast buffet glistened with fresh fruit, pastries, and an omelette station. Freshly ground coffee was brewing.

SUZANNE: Tommy, this is fabulous. You're a master of detail.

TOMMY: I'm a gay man, Suzanne. Over-the-top elegance is a minimum requirement.

[We laughed]

SUZANNE: Any tips on how to make today a success?

TOMMY: Well, you met everyone yesterday – the good, the bad, and the ugly. Other than a makeover for the ugly, I have no recommendations. You'll do fine, really. They're wonderful people. Forgive me, please. I need to get to the office. Karen should be here momentarily. Here's my cell if you need anything.

[Tommy bowed slightly as he handed me his card. He made a crisp turn and was gone.]

[I had a few minutes to gaze at the fog over the bay before Karen arrived. She was happy and optimistic.]

KAREN: I'm so, so relieved that things went well with Randall yesterday. I got an email from him last night that he found some leadership courses at UC Berkeley, and he asked if he could talk with you about long-term coaching. What a turn around. And, then this morning. My gosh, I have to tell you what happened in the parking lot…Oh, good morning, Jasmine. You met Suzanne yesterday, didn't you?

While her managers enjoyed breakfast, Karen briefly introduced me to the group. I began by explaining The Mind to Lead Attunement Model and the retreat goal of using power appropriately. Over the course of the day, through lecturettes, case studies, exercises, and role plays, I would share how each of the seven Influence Tools can help a mindful leader use power appropriately. We started with **Laser Messages.**

LASER MESSAGES

"Do you know anyone at work who talks too much?" I asked the group. There was laughter and a few nods at each other across the tables. "When a person talks too much, it's not only boring. It's hard to know what's most important in their message. Instead of confusing your listener, when you want to make a strong impact, try *speaking* in a single sentence. It not only saves time and *focuses* the other person's mind on your expectation, it also *focuses* your mind."

"Speaking in short sentences is important," I continued, "because a leader's goal is to keep the conversation firmly on the expectation highway headed straight to your destination. When you add unnecessary details or talk too much, it's like constructing an exit ramp, so that your employee, boss, or customer has an escape route. Don't give the other person an opening to detour the conversation. State your concern or expectation and nothing more. That's why coaches call this tool Laser Messaging; it *focuses* all minds on the issue like a laser beam."

I asked the group to brainstorm some Laser Messages that describe the most common employee behavior problems. They created:

- **TARDINESS**: "You've been more than 30 minutes late three times this month."
- **POOR PERFORMANCE**: "Your error rate on data entry has gone above the acceptable limit."
- **BAD ATTITUDE**: "When you complain, it slows down team meetings."

Their examples described undesirable behaviors. While a corrective Laser Message always refers to a behavior, you can vary the level of specificity depending on various factors such as the person's overall job performance, how long her behavior has been a problem, and her relative responsiveness to other corrective conversations about this or other behaviors in the past. A general rule of thumb is – the bigger the problem or the more resistance you expect, the more specific you can be in describing the behavior. The first example above is the most specific in that it describes the duration and frequency of tardiness.

If, on the other hand, you're talking with a good employee who has strayed slightly off the path, you can deliver a broader statement for her to interpret. The last message in the list is the most general. It allows the employee to think about what she's doing that's unacceptable and how she can modify her behavior.

In addition to corrective comments, you can also use all of the Influence Tools to deliver positive feedback or to coach high-performers. The group generated several Laser Messages for acknowledging good performance including:

- **PERFECT ATTENDANCE:** "You made a Herculean effort to cover the Help Desk this quarter."
- **OUTSTANDING PERFORMANCE:** "You're the Wizard of Pods; thanks for erecting the cubicles so quickly."
- **TREMENDOUS ATTITUDE:** "Could we inject everyone on the team with DNA from your enthusiasm?"

After the group finished writing a list of positive messages, Ravi, the head of the pediatric pharmaceuticals lab, raised his hand.

> RAVI: Those are silly. I'd never say anything so ridiculous. And, I can't always talk in one sentence at a time. I have complex ideas to communicate. This just won't work.

> SUZANNE: Thanks for being honest, Ravi. You're expressing two valid concerns. You want to come across as authentic. And, you want your communication to be thorough. Are those accurate summaries?

> RAVI: Yes, those are the problems I have with these Laser Message statements. They don't feel right.

> SUZANNE: Who else has a concern about Laser Messages?

> [Juan and Randall raised their hands.]

> JUAN: I agree with Ravi. My employees need more information. Particularly when I'm explaining a new procedure.

> [Randall nodded his head in agreement.]

> SUZANNE: Thanks for your comments, Ravi and Juan. Let me clarify. I'm not suggesting that you only *speak* in single sentences. That would be impossible and ineffective. Most conversations are a relaxed give and take where it's good to be relatively succinct, however you wouldn't want to limit yourself to single sentences. Laser Messages are like a spice. You use them sparingly and strategically in verbal and written communication. It's an Influence Tool that

focuses the listener's mind on a specific issue or outcome.

[Though Karen had been quiet up until now, she jumped in to offer an example.]

KAREN: Lasering has helped me develop concise, accurate messages for my meetings with Gary. You all know how busy he is
with the reorg and new plants in Europe. He told me last month
that all he can give me for the next two quarters is a 20-minute
meeting once a week. That's it. So, I write my agenda in six to eight
laser statements, email it to him 24 hours in advance, and we jump
right into it when I walk in the door. He really appreciates it and
told me that he's going to ask all of his Division Directors to use
the same format.

The group listened intently, and a few nodded their heads in agreement. Then, Suzie, the youngest manager in the group and head of the autoimmune diagnostics lab spoke up.

SUZIE: Does he talk in Laser? Because, I can't see Gary being brief!

[The room erupted in laughter.]

KAREN: Actually, Suzie, he's getting better. He goes down my
laser list and approves a lot of my ideas and requests quickly. Of
course, some of them we discuss in great detail, and sometimes
those conversations get a bit heated. Overall, though, he's getting
more concise, because he just doesn't have time to chat anymore.

SUZANNE: Thanks for sharing that example, Karen. Would any of
you like to experiment with a similar laser list for your next one-
on-one with Karen?

Three managers raised their hand. Karen nodded a "thank you" to each one and noted their names.

I wanted to give people the opportunity to deliver a Laser Message during a conversation to see how it felt. I passed around instructions for role-plays, and the group

broke into trios to practice them.

SUZANNE: What did you learn about Laser Messages?

JASMINE: Because they're short, they're potent. Sort of like a double dark chocolate brownie. They take extra time to digest, if you will. Particularly with the negative Laser, I found myself **pausing** after I said it, so that Bob could take it in.

SUZANNE: Yes, thank you, Jasmine. Coaches describe the pause after a strong message as a time for "letting it land." Wait as long as needed for the other person to absorb and respond to your message. Think of the pause as a form of communication. Even by delivering silence, you remain an active participant in the conversation.

JUAN: I hate silence.

SUZANNE: That's normal. Who else feels uncomfortable with silence?

[Everyone except Suzie raised a hand.]

SUZANNE: After delivering a strong message, it's common to feel concerned about how it was received. During the pause, I would invite you to feel the sensations in your body, and to reflect on, "What's the power of a silent pause?"

MARK: My pause gives the receiver the time and space to not only take in and decode the meaning of my message, but to formulate a reasoned response. I got to practice this last month during a difficult situation with Dana. In the past, I would disrupt her processing time with my nervous static like, "What I meant was…." or "I hope you don't take this personally. I think you're doing a great job. It's just that your behavior…." All of those extra comments distracted her mind from my original message. By being afraid to pause, I kept giving her more brownies – using Jasmine's analogy – to digest.

Mark explained how Karen trained him to stay relaxed during the pause. When he started to feel tense and compelled to speak, he stopped himself and moved his awareness into the tension. It was in his throat and chest. He just sat there feeling the constriction and taking deep breaths. It was hard to do. However, the results were excellent. He stopped his pattern of trying to save Dana by jumping in with an answer for her problem. When he was quiet, she had to come up with her own solution. The pause worked beautifully. And, he learned that he won't die from not speaking.

> BOB: I learned the same thing from raising four kids. If I do all the talking, I never find out what's going on in their minds. As my wife says, "Give the gift of silence."

> JASMINE: What do you do if you're just a natural interrupter? I have a bad habit of finishing people's sentences.

> SUZANNE: Jasmine, you've taken the first step in changing that behavior, simply by being aware of it. Here's a tip that might help. When you pause, gently place your tongue against the back of your front teeth; it's harder to speak from that position. Can everyone get a feel for that?

I watched as they tried the technique and nodded in agreement.

Before we took a break, I summarized the first two tools. Delivering a Laser Message is like pointing to a file and saying, "Let's open this file, and work in here." Delivering a Pause is like giving the person time to look inside the file, review the contents, and form a response. Her initial response will move the conversation in one of three directions: forward, backward, or nowhere. Conversations are like a chess match. Her move influences your next move.

People nodded their heads in agreement. So, I asked the group to be back in ten minutes.

Karen walked up to me with a Cheshire cat grin.

> KAREN: It's going great. Everyone is participating. And, you won't believe what happened in the parking lot this morning when I

parked next to Randall. He walked over as I was getting out of my car and said, "Are we going to talk at the retreat today about our conversation yesterday?" I said, "No, absolutely not, Randall. That's a private personnel matter. I would never mention that." He looked disappointed and said, "Could I bring it up if it feels appropriate?" I asked, "What would you like to bring up?" He said, "I might want to talk about how you helped me solve a long-standing professional problem. Are you okay with me bringing that up, because, Karen, I really appreciated your help and felt you did an excellent job in our conversation." Suzanne, I think my eyes popped out of my head. It was great. I told him he could bring up whatever he wanted to. Is that okay?

SUZANNE: Hmm. Let's think through this. It's exciting that he appreciated your help and wants to acknowledge his insights. What possible problems could arise from his disclosure?

KAREN: He might regret it in the morning. And, he's not exactly the darling of the management team. He might be on a high right now, but I'd hate for people to throw this back at him when he backslides.

SUZANNE: Good points. How could you support him to self-disclose in a safe way?

KAREN: I'm going to talk with him right now. I'll ask some Open-Ended Questions to help him think through the possible outcomes of different levels of disclosure. Thanks, Suzanne.

At the end of the break, Karen walked into the meeting room behind Randall. She flashed me a thumbs up, so I knew we were in good shape.

FACTS & FEELINGS

After welcoming the group back, I explained the third Influence Tool, **Facts & Feelings**. It's a special Laser Message that reflects back a person's feelings about a situation.

Some leaders are uncomfortable with Facts & Feelings, because they think it's fake or manipulative. One reason people don't like the tool is because it was used inappropriately on them. I asked who that had happened to.

JANICE: That would be me. When my mother broke her hip and had to have emergency surgery, the techs screwed up the amount of one of her blood transfusions. I was livid and frankly, I sort of lost it. One of the nurses pulled me aside and said, "You feel upset, because your elderly mother is in poor health." If my husband hadn't been there, I would have killed her.

SUZANNE: Janice, that sounds like a deeply disturbing experience. On top of your emotional trauma, someone misused Facts & Feelings. Everyone, what was wrong with the statement?

JASMINE: It was inaccurate. Janice wasn't upset about her mother's health. She was angry, and justifiably so, at the hospital's incompetence.

SUZANNE: Exactly. When using this tool, don't pick the facts that you like. Reflect what the person is truly upset or concerned about, or in positive cases, happy about. Anything else about Janice's example that we can learn from?

SUZIE: Even if the nurse had gotten it right, should she have used this tool in a life-threatening and possibly litigious situation? Janice could have sued the hospital for malpractice.

SUZANNE: It's a good question, Suzie. Unfortunately, there's no rule book on when to use a tool or not. Janice, what do you wish the nurse had said?

JANICE: I would have liked, "Mrs. Frederick, the blood technician made a big mistake. I want to assure you, though, that your mother is not in danger because of it. How can I best support your family right now?" As Suzie pointed out though, the nurse probably wouldn't admit to a mistake.

SUZANNE: Thank you, Janice. What is, "The blood technician made a big mistake"?

RANDALL: It's just the facts.

JUAN: Without the feelings. Is that okay to use half of the equation?

SUZANNE: Yes. That's all Janice wanted. Sometimes, the tool feels more authentic – for the sender and receiver – if you use only one piece of the formula.

JUST THE FACTS

I thanked Janice for sharing a good illustration of a bad Facts & Feelings. Then, I asked the group to work in pairs, and write statements about work situations that reflected only the facts. Here are some statements they wrote that show a mindful leader understands the situation:

- "It sounds like you want an improved work flow procedure."
- "I get the sense that you have higher expectations of your team members than they have of each other."
- "I think you want help prioritizing these tasks."

We discussed how whenever you reflect back to someone, it's always a guess. To communicate that your message is conjecture not conclusion, use a neutral or even questioning tone of voice. Or, add a qualifier at the end of your statement such as, "Did I get that right?" or "Is that it?"

FEELINGS, NOTHING MORE THAN FEELINGS

If the other person is having a strong emotion or doesn't seem to be aware of how her feelings are impacting her behavior, I explained to the group how to reflect back only the feeling. Here are some of the statements they wrote that show a leader empathizes with the situation:

- "That's so frustrating."
- "You're disappointed, is that right?"
- "Sounds like you're angry."

UNDERSTAND AND EMPATHIZE

After the group finished writing statements, I summarized the tool.

SUZANNE: When you combine Facts and Feelings, you get a more precise hypothesis, for example, "I think you're upset (the feeling), because you want more information about who'll be moved to the other department (the fact)." Reflecting back both the facts and feelings also helps the other person feel heard which may lead her to talk more about the issue. Who has any questions or comments about this tool before we move on to the next one?

JUAN: I don't have time to do therapy on people.

SUZANNE: Thanks for your honesty, Juan. It sounds like you're frustrated with this tool, because you don't want to spend your day listening to people whine and complain. Is that right?

JUAN: Yes, it is. I've got too much to do, and, frankly, I don't care how people feel. I want them to get their work done.

SUZANNE: I hear you. You were hired to run a lab, not to deal with people's feelings. And, it's irritating to have this new expectation put on you.

JUAN: Yes. I am irritated. This wasn't in my job description. And, I don't see the value in it.

SUZIE: May I interrupt? Has anyone noticed that Suzanne is using Facts & Feelings on Juan, and pretty successfully, I might add. Each time she uses it, I notice him relaxing a bit more and giving her more information.

Juan's forehead tightened as he reflected on Suzie's comments.

JUAN: Hmm, I guess you're right, Suzie. I didn't even notice. Okay, point taken, Suzanne. I see how the tool works.

SUZANNE: Thanks, Suzie. Juan, I'm with you. I don't want you to listen to complainers all day. However, if a person's upset amygdala is holding her rational prefrontal cortex hostage, she isn't getting much work done anyway.

RANDALL: Suzanne, if I may. I had the same reaction to this tool as you, Juan, until yesterday. I don't need to go into a whole lot of detail except to say that I communicated inappropriately about a team member in a meeting that Karen and Suzanne were observing. This group knows me, so I don't need to...Well, I'll just tell you. I referred to a team member in the room as a kid. After the meeting, Karen called me into her office, I assumed, to read me the riot act. But, that's not what happened.

[Randall looked at Karen as he continued.]

RANDALL: You stayed calm. Maybe a better word is neutral. You used Facts & Feelings to uncover the root problem in my behavior. The tool removed you from our conversation, and put the focus on me. You're right, Suzanne, that stating a few details from a situation not only calmed me down, it engaged my neocortex in problem-solving.

KAREN: Randall, thanks for sharing your experience and for acknowledging my role.

I thanked the group for the excellent questions and insights. Then, I summarized what we had covered: how to write a Laser Message, how to Pause after you deliver it, and how to use Facts & Feelings to reflect what's going on in a situation. I distributed a handout with an exercise they could do on their own or with a colleague to practice the three tools. (You can find this exercise at themindtolead.com.) We had one more tool to cover before lunch that we had already touched on a bit.

VENTING

I explained to the group that as a leader begins to surface a performance problem using the first three skills, it's common that the person you're helping might resist by complaining. Due to the natural negativity of the brain, complaining is a normal and sometimes helpful phase in a solution-oriented conversation. **Venting** – or as a colleague refers to it, a Beef, Moan, and Whine (BMW) session – may help a person express rather than repress negative thoughts and feelings, and then move on to a new level of action. Here are some suggested guidelines for Venting.

Given the chance to complain, some people will decline, while others will cautiously share. Others will jump at the chance to vent. For people who are comfortable Venting, set specific boundaries about time, language, and volume.

Set a Venting time limit. I recommend up to five minutes. The average person should be able to express a complaint in a few minutes. If she can't, then teach her Laser Messaging. Let the person know that you are setting a timer or keeping an eye on the clock.

Be clear about what is acceptable language. In my opinion, profanity is inappropriate in the workplace. Some leaders disagree. A few clients have told me that they don't mind swearing as long as it's not targeted toward people. In other words, if a person wants to curse about a software program or changes in the benefit package, some leaders aren't offended. Know your standards, communicate them clearly, and hold people to them.

Also, be clear about the acceptable volume for Venting. Some people like to shout or pound a desk. While some leaders are okay with loud, I don't recommend being that liberal. It teaches a person that when she's angry, it's acceptable to yell or get physical. I feel it's more productive to use words to express strong feelings. In order to do that, some people need help increasing their emotional fluency. Distribute copies of the Feelings List in the Appendix to people who want to boost their emotional vocabulary.

DISCOMFORT WITH EXPRESSING FEELINGS

Keep in mind that while some people can vent all day, others are uncomfortable complaining or talking about their concerns. Some people believe that feelings are private and shouldn't be shared, particularly at work. Others believe that having negative feelings is inherently wrong, so discussing those feelings only highlights a personal flaw.

When you sense that a person is resistant to talking about their concerns, find a neutral way to *speak* about it: "This assignment is hard enough, and now I'm asking you to talk about how it bothers you. This must be a challenging conversation." If the person is very private, don't expect a big breakthrough. You may *observe* a wide range of responses, ranging from a quiet "yes," to rolling eyes, or an angry stare. Accept those responses as an expression of emotion.

Another way to reduce a person's resistance to expressing concerns is to role model it. Self-disclosure shows the kinds of appropriate words, body language, and intensity to use when describing emotions. As the other person *observes* your role modeling, it engages her brain's mirror neurons that help her mimic behavior (see **Mind Trick Box** on **MIRROR NEURONS**).

MIND TRICK BOX
| MIRROR NEURONS: MONKEY SEE, MONKEY DO

The brain is a social organ. One aspect of its social nature was discovered in Italy in the 1990s when scientists placed electrodes in the inferior frontal cortex of macaque monkeys. Researchers wanted to study the neural control of monkeys' hands as they grabbed and manipulated objects. The scientists, Giacomo Rizzolatti and Vittorio Gallese, found that mirror neurons in the frontal cortex fired when the monkeys performed tasks, but they also fired when the monkeys watched someone else perform the same specific tasks (Iacoboni 2008).

Recent imaging and behavioral studies strongly suggest that the human inferior frontal cortex and superior parietal lobe, which closely match those studied in the macaque monkey, respond during both action and observation of the action. Mirror neurons are helping scientists understand a variety of amazing human skills such as imitation, empathy, mind reading, and language acquisition. Some researchers hypothesize that mental deficits like autism might stem from damages in mirror neurons (Iacobini 2008).

When you role model, be authentic and *speak* about your own resistance to expressing feelings. "I'm still learning how to do this, so it might come across as awkward. I want to try to describe right now how I'm responding to your performance. [Pause] I'm frustrated about your absences and unsure about your job commitment." Then, Pause again, and *observe* how she responds.

If she doesn't use feeling words, that's fine. Move back to *focusing* on your behavioral expectation. Don't push it. You can return to the topic in subsequent conversations, particularly if the individual's lack of emotion regulation impacts a job competency such as teamwork or attitude. Of course, it's okay to drop the issue entirely. You can't force a person to develop emotional intelligence at work.

I asked the group for two volunteers to demonstrate a successful Venting conversation. Suzie and Bob raised their hands. Suzie wanted to practice staying open and calm while holding a slightly challenging person to the established venting ground rules. Bob agreed to help out by breaking a few of the rules. Suzie started out in a relaxed posture as she listened to Bob's complaints. However, as the conversation continued and he began to repeat himself, Suzie's breathing quickened and her shoulders tensed up.

SUZIE: He's turning into a broken record.

[The group laughed.]

SUZANNE: Oops, I forgot to include an important Venting ground rule. One mention per complaint. Let's hear you explain that boundary to Bob.

SUZIE: Excuse me, Bob. I can hear that you're upset about several steps in the delivery process. You've mentioned that three times. I want you to know that I've heard that complaint and how irritated you are. And, I'd like to make a request. For the remainder of this period of Venting, by the way you've got two minutes left, as well as any Venting sessions we have in the future, I want to ask that you state each unique complaint only once.

BOB: Why?

SUZIE: Because I said so! (Laughter) Actually, Bob, I'm glad you asked. What do you see as the benefits of making each complaint just once?

BOB: Hmm. I'll have to listen to myself. And, maybe I'll see that there aren't that many different things to complain about. I guess that would make it easier to come up with a solution.

SUZIE (Looking over her shoulder at me and beaming): I like this rule, Suzanne.

SUZANNE: Expert job explaining it, Suzie. And, masterful work letting Bob answer his own question. You did that by switching from the Tell to the Ask approach and by asking an Open-Ended Question, which, by the way, is the first skill we'll cover this afternoon. Now, it's time for us to head over to the library for lunch. Thank you all very much for your participation this morning.

As Karen and I walked to lunch, we debriefed the morning.

KAREN: People are telling me the role-plays are very helpful. They love getting practice and feedback. And, oh, I just got a text from Tommy, "Reminder gardens exquisite." Will we have time to walk through them after lunch?

SUZANNE: If the weather holds, I'd like to do an exercise in the garden this afternoon.

KAREN: Great.

OPEN-ENDED QUESTIONS

I began the afternoon session with a question.

SUZANNE: When you encounter someone who is resistant, what's your natural inclination?

JANICE: I wish I could say I'm open-minded. The truth is, I usually tense up and resist back. I become more directive to make sure they get the message.

SUZANNE: I see several people nodding in agreement, though not you, Bob.

BOB: If telling people what to do worked, none of us would be here. I just finished reading Howard Gardner's book, *Changing*

Minds: The Art and Science of Changing Our Own and Other People's Minds (Gardner 2004). He says the best way to change a mind is to reduce the person's resistance. To do that, you have to find out what the opposition is about. So, when I encounter a resistant person, I try to be curious and ask a lot of questions.

SUZANNE: Questions are often a good strategy, Bob. When mindful leaders use a particular kind of question that I mentioned before lunch – Open-Ended Questions – they show interest and elicit information.

I explained the differences between Open-Ended and closed-ended questions. Open-Ended Questions begin with five words that reporters use to capture key facts:

- Who
- What
- When
- Where
- How

Closed-ended questions, on the other hand, usually begin with words like "Have you," "Did you," "Could you," or "Are you." Because closed-ended questions can only be answered with "Yes" or "No," they don't elicit much new information or encourage new thinking. Notice how these closed questions are simply suggestions or commands with a question mark on the end.

- "Have you talked with the customer to get another perspective?"
- "Did you do an Internet search on the competition?"
- "Are you going to think of another way to do this?"

Another weakness of many closed-ended questions is that they usually elicit the "right" answer rather an honest response. For example, after you delegate a task and ask, "Do you understand?," the direct report will usually give the answer that she thinks is correct, which is, "Yes." While she probably does understand, the likelihood that she understands everything exactly as you want it to be remembered and acted upon may not be very high. When you ask closed questions, it might seem like you're saving time by getting to the point or the "right" answer. In reality, you're limiting your ability to find out what's really going on in the other person's mind. You need information, not head bobbing. As a result, you don't get any information about the resistance, which is what you need to know in order to change her mind. I asked what questions the group had so far.

RAVI: Why isn't "Why" on the list?

MARK: It's interrogative.

SUZANNE: Exactly. Who used to ask, "Why did you do that?," and in some cases, still does?

[A couple people blurted out "Mom" amid laughter.]

SUZANNE: When someone on your team delivers an unexpected outcome, sometimes referred to as a "mistake," there's a tendency to want to ask, "Why did you do that?" However, how effective is that question? First, people often don't know why they did something. Second, asking the question can lead to some pretty wild stories along the lines of, "My dog ate my homework."

[Ravi and Randall were shaking their heads in disagreement.]

RANDALL: You're being cavalier, Suzanne. I can't just overlook a mistake. It's my responsibility to assure that it doesn't happen again. I don't think you understand that in our work, lives are at stake.

BOB: She's not saying that, Randall. You can still ask questions about how something went awry. She's just saying that interrogating people doesn't help.

SUZANNE: Thanks, Bob. Randall, you're right. You are responsible for assuring that errors are fixed and not repeated. Let's try something as a group. Give me five different Open-Ended Questions that you could ask instead of, "Why did you do that?" Let's use each word on the list.

People called out the following questions:

- "Who influenced the plan you developed?"
- "What steps did you take to get to this outcome?"
- "When did you see the first signs that this might not turn out as you had hoped?"
- "Where did you go for data to support your approach?"
- "How did you test the process before implementing it?"

> RANDALL: Okay, Suzanne. Now I see what you're talking about. These questions would solicit much more information than "Why did you do that?"

> SUZANNE: Thanks, Randall. Ravi, how are you feeling about letting go of "Why"?

> Ravi nodded his head "yes."

Leaders tell me that the two most challenging Influence Tools to use are also the most valuable: Laser Messages and Open-Ended Questions. These tools sum up Tell versus Ask. Use them like a good traffic cop. Laser Messages are like holding up your palm, and telling people to stop and pay attention. Open-Ended Questions are like motioning people forward, and asking for solutions to the problem. The next Influence Tool is a combination of stop and go.

BEER, THE FEEDBACK/REQUEST FORMULA

I explained to the group that if they use all of the previous Influence Tools in a challenging conversation and still feel that they're not reaching their goal, then **BEER** could be helpful (Figure 6.3). BEER is a four-step feedback/request formula that adds to the two steps in Facts & Feelings. In addition to describing the behavior [Facts] and your emotion [Feelings] about it, BEER includes the impact of the person's behavior and a specific request.

BEER is a combination of Ask and Tell. In steps 1 through 3, BEER, lets you Tell the other person how her behavior impacts you and/or others. Then, depending on the situation, BEER lets you either Ask a specific request or Tell a job directive.

I developed BEER based on assertiveness training courses that I've taken and presented over the last 25 years as well as on the work of Marshall B. Rosenberg and

The Center for Nonviolent Communication, cnvc.org. I highly recommend Marshall's book, *Nonviolent Communication: A Language of Life* (Rosenberg 2003). You can listen to a radio interview I did with him at goodradioshows.org; click on Peace Talks Episodes in 2006.

FIGURE 6.3 BEER FEEDBACK/REQUEST FORMULA

STEP	LANGUAGE
1. BEHAVIOR (Facts)	When you _____
2. EFFECT	The impact on (clients, the team, you, etc.) is _____
3. EMOTION (Feelings)	I feel _____
4. REQUEST/REQUIREMENT	I request/require that you _____

My formula differs from Marshall's in three significant ways, because BEER:

• Was designed for the workplace. Marshall's model was developed for all settings.

• Describes the Effect that the Behavior has on other people and/or the organization. Marshall's model, instead, describes how the behavior relates to an unmet need.

• Offers the option to (1) make a Request, or (2) if the sender is the receiver's boss, state a job Requirement. In Marshall's model, the sender always makes a request.

When people first learn it, some think the BEER formula is too rigid. However, over time, most people say that using a formula to deliver difficult feedback is better than winging it during the conversation. Without a formula, there's a tendency to talk too much or feel unsure about what to say next.

I explained to Karen's group that they might only need to use one or two of the steps in order to receive a positive response. However, sometimes a situation requires all four steps. I briefly described each step and suggestions for delivering them in the case of constructive performance feedback, in other words when something unacceptable is happening.

1. Describe the **behavior** that you're dissatisfied with. Deliver a Laser Message that describes either the person's unacceptable existing behavior or the lack of a productive behavior. It should be a precise report of a measurable behavior. For example, "You've been twenty minutes late to work every day for two weeks." Describe the behavior without being judgmental. For example, the statement, "You're not committed to your job," doesn't make sense to an employee, because she feels very committed to her job. She doesn't understand why you think that her arriving twenty minutes late means that she's disloyal. She might be having problems with childcare or one of her elderly parents. It's more helpful for her when you simply describe the behavior that you're disappointed with rather than interpret the cause.

2. Explain the **effect** of the behavior. Describe how her behavior impacts you, the team, the organization, or a combination of these. State the effect in one sentence, for example, "I can't open the customer service desk, so customers are dissatisfied." This step reminds her that she is part of a team or process that relies on her.

3. State your **emotion** about the situation. In one sentence, tell her how you feel. Use a variation on one or more of the four universal emotions:
- Mad
- Sad
- Glad
- Afraid

For example, "I feel really frustrated," "I'm concerned," or "I'm angry." These are different flavors of the universal emotion, "Mad." Refer to the Feelings List in the Appendix for help selecting the best word in one of these categories. Remember that, "I feel like you're not committed" or "I feel like firing you" don't describe an emotion. Those are judgments.

4. Make a specific **request**. The request states how you want her to behave in the

future. It should be a SMART goal: Specific, Measurable, Attainable, Realistic, and Time-oriented. Unless it's a job requirement, put your request in the form of an Open-Ended Question: "What will it take for you to be sitting at the receptionist desk no later than 8 a.m. every day for the next five work days?"

In most cases, your request should cover a relatively short time frame. Avoid requests like, "What needs to change so that you are on time for work every day?" That's too open-ended and difficult to track, much less achieve. Make a request that's realistic; for some of your employees, that covers the next day or the next week. Schedule a follow-up meeting to check progress on the behavior. Help the employee to win small rather than lose big.

Realize that if it was easy for her to get to work on time, she'd already be doing it. Making a behavioral shift usually takes some detective work to find out what's getting in the way. After you make the request, pause and wait for her response. If she's silent or resistant, use Open-Ended Questions to help her analyze barriers, and plan for a successful outcome. Here are some examples:

- "What are the barriers to getting to work on time?"
- "What changes will you make to be able to consistently arrive on time?"
- "How will you track your success with this behavior?"

Now that you know the four BEER steps, here are some delivery tips for making the conversation go smoothly.

PAUSE BETWEEN EACH STEP

Remember that you might not need to use all four steps. Deliver the steps one at a time, and look for possible exit ramps or opportunities to leave the BEER formula and move into a collaborative, problem-solving mode. Let's look at the exit ramps after each step.

After you describe the behavior in step one, "You've been 10 minutes late to work every day for two weeks," pause and wait for her response. Be silent. Try counting to five or even ten. With that much silence, your employee may become uncomfortable, and she may talk to fill in the space.

If she responds to your description of the behavior, listen for clues. She might offer an explanation like, "I'm having car problems. I've been trying to catch the bus, but it's always late." This is the first possible exit ramp from the BEER formula toward negotiating a resolution. As you exit BEER, ask a question that moves her mind into problem-solving: "What are some solutions to your transportation issues?"

However, instead of seeing an exit ramp, you might get a blank stare or an unconvincing response like, "I know" or "I'll take care of it." In that case, calmly move to step two: explain the effect. "When you're late, I have to pull somebody else off the floor to cover customer service." Then, pause and wait. If there's no response, you can move on to the emotion or stick with effect by engaging her input through a question. You could ask, "How do you think your behavior is impacting the team?"

If you're getting through to her, she might respond with "I'm sorry that it's affecting the team. I know people are angry with me. They're ignoring me." Let her talk about how her behavior impacts the team and how they're treating her. Most teams won't let poor performance go unnoticed. If she agrees with you or admits that something's wrong, it's another possible exit ramp from the BEER formula and a move toward resolution.

TALKING ABOUT FEELINGS SHIFTS A CONVERSATION

However, if you get a shoulder shrug or a deer-in-the-headlights stare, then state your emotion with, "I'm concerned that you're not tuned into your team" or something shorter like, "I'm frustrated." Laser it. Don't go on and on, and don't whine at her with, "You've changed. Your attitude has dropped. I've received so many complaints about you…" When you whine, you role model, "Whining is how we communicate here. As soon as I finish whining, then you're going to whine back at me." Instead of teaching her to whine, show her how to be calm, honest, and concise. Remember to use "I" rather than "you" at the beginning of a feeling statement. Avoid statements like, "You're making me angry." The employee isn't making you mad. She is choosing behaviors that you're responding to with an unpleasant emotion, because you want her to act in a different way. Role model how to talk about and own your feelings rather than blaming your reactions on other people.

Be prepared that when you state your feeling, the person may respond with an apology, "I'm really sorry I acted that way." An apology is a definite exit ramp to move onto the solution highway. If, however, there's no response to your silence, you have the option to ask a question about emotion for example, "What's your response to that feeling?" or "How do you feel about your behavior?"

MAKE A SPECIFIC REQUEST

If, at this point in the formula, you're not seeing some movement toward collaboration, go to the fourth step, which is making a specific request. "How can you commit to being at the receptionist desk no later than 8 a.m. every day for the next week?"

Some leaders, particularly people with a Leading style, don't like the word "request." They feel, based on their position of power, that the fourth step should state a "requirement." If you prefer to state requirements, I recommend that you use them sparingly and only at the level of verbal and written warnings.

I prefer calling the fourth step a request, because it lets the employee make a choice. If the employee isn't willing to meet some of your requests, then it's your job to communicate that she might not be a good fit for the job. I'm not saying that every time she does something poorly that you should threaten to fire her. I'm suggesting that if you see a pattern over several weeks or a month of her being unaccountable to your requests, then it's time to talk about whether she's in the right place or not. Remember, if telling people what to do (requirement) worked, you wouldn't have any performance problems in the first place.

After making your request, pause. If she doesn't offer a response, ask a question. Avoid close-ended questions like, "Can you do that?" because, she'd most likely say, "Yes." If you ask, "Do you have any questions?" she'd probably say, "No." Instead, ask an Open-Ended Question such as, "What's the first step you're going to take?" or "How can I help you be successful with this new behavior?"

EMPLOYEES ARE RESPONSIBLE FOR TRACKING THEIR PROGRESS

When you make a request that an employee agrees to, it's her responsibility, not yours, to track her performance improvement. Emphasize to the employee, "Reporting back to me is part of this behavioral expectation. How and when will you update me on your progress?"

If the employee doesn't perform well or doesn't report back, it's important to have a follow-up conversation about this right away. If she continues to fall short on your expectations over weeks or months, it's appropriate to take the next step of a verbal warning or to initiate a disciplinary action. I know you don't want to come across as harsh. However, assertive, precise, and firm are very different from cruel. When an employee isn't meeting your minimum expectations, don't let it slide.

In summary, instead of wasting valuable time with arguing or avoiding challenging situations, BEER offers a calm, direct communication formula. Addressing and resolving problems can help you feel less stressed and get better results.

FLEXING YOUR STYLE

After I gave the group time to practice writing and delivering BEER statements, we moved into the last Influence Tool: flexing your approach to handle different communication styles and each style's unique form of resistance.

Style typing began in ancient times. Astrology was one of the first systems for explaining differences. By 400 BC, the Greek philosopher Hippocrates developed a new typing approach based on the fluid in a person's body.

He said that a choleric person has a cold fast fluid and is direct and decisive; this makes her a good leader. A sanguine type has a fast warm fluid that could bubble out of the mouth making her talk a lot and be social. A melancholy type has a slow, cold fluid that focuses her mind on thinking and details. A phlegmatic person has warm slow fluid that makes her stable, relational, and a good team player.

Fast forward to the 20th century, when many behavioral scientists like Carl Jung refined Hippocrates' theory. Jung identified four psychological functions – thinking, feeling, sensation, and intuition – and, he classified people as either "introverted" or "extroverted." Assessments such as the Myers-Briggs Type Indicator, DISC Personality System, and Social Styles questionnaire use his functions and classifications to identify an individual's temperament.

FIGURE 6.4 FOUR STYLES

STYLES	TASK FOCUS (COLD)	PEOPLE FOCUS (WARM)
EXTROVERT (FAST)	Leading (choleric)	Socializing (sanguine)
INTROVERT (SLOW)	Thinking (melancholy)	Relating (phlegmatic)

FOUR STYLES

I often use style assessments to help team members become more mindful and understanding of each other's strengths and gaps. Even if you don't have access to a style assessment, you can probably make a good guess about a person's primary style by using mindfulness and this table (Figure 6.4). When you want to improve your communication with someone, first, ask yourself two questions: "Is this person more an extrovert or an introvert?" And, "When she speaks, does she tend to talk more about task or people issues?"

As I drew a large rectangle on the flip chart pad and divided it into nine equal cells, Karen raised her hand.

> KAREN: Suzanne, don't we have to be careful about stereotyping people?

> SUZANNE: Yes, it's an important point. While many people tend to have a primary style that's stronger than the others, most of us are a mixture of two or more of these four basic styles. So, it's helpful not to assume that a person will always operate from one style.

> JASMINE: Are you saying that we should change our style to match another person's style?

> SUZANNE: Not exactly. Otherwise, we would all just be flipping to the other person's style and not much would change in terms of resistance. Keep in mind that in addition to acting in a certain way, each style has a particular way of showing resistance that can be an exaggeration of the style's qualities. For example, have you noticed that people who like to talk – the Socializer type – often show resistance by talking even more?

> JANICE: Definitely.

> SUZANNE: Which of the tools we've learned today could be helpful with a Socializer?

> MARK: I'd use a Laser Message to shorten the conversation and *focus* the person's mind on one issue.

> JUAN: [Facts & Feelings] Something like, "You must be upset about XYZ issue." Could that help the person get back to work?

SUZANNE: Yes, possibly. Any other tools that might be useful with a talkative person?

SUZIE: I'd ask an Open-Ended Question. Something with a time frame, for example, "When can you have this finished?"

SUZANNE: Good examples, everyone. You understand how to lessen resistance with a Socializer by being mindful, first, of what she says that begins to derail the conversation and, second, of what you ask or tell to put it back on track. Now, I want you to work in greater depth on all of the styles. I have four case studies about resistant people – one case on each style. I'd like you to work in pairs. Each pair will take one of these case study packets that include instructions. In 45 minutes, your team will present its case to the group including a brief summary of the style, a list of ways to motivate the style, and a demo conversation on how to mindfully reduce resistance from the style. It's a beautiful afternoon, so feel free to work outside if you like. We'll meet in the garden at 3:30 for group presentations. Since we have an extra person, Karen has offered to float among the pairs and offer help. I'll stay here in the meeting room if you have any questions. Have fun!

CASE STUDIES: FOUR STYLES OF RESISTANCE

Forty minutes later, when I walked out to the gazebo, there were ten comfortable chairs arranged in a circle for us. Two servers were setting up lemonade and soft drinks with chips and guacamole. Within a few minutes, the pairs began arriving.

RANDALL: Jasmine and I had the hardest case study.

JUAN: I doubt that. Wait 'til you see Janice's character. She's a tough one to influence.

SUZANNE: Welcome back, everyone. I'm excited to hear your presentations and find out what you learned about reducing resistance. As you listen to each style description and demo conversation, think of someone you work with who has that style. Imagine yourself using the suggested communication techniques when speaking with that person. Who wants to go first?

BOB: We will. Mark and I had the Leader style.

SUZIE: Can Ravi and I go second? We're the Socializer case.

SUZANNE: Sounds good. Let's get started.

HELP THE LEADER ZOOM IN

Bob and Mark began their presentation by explaining that the Leader style is a task-oriented extrovert.

MARK: A Leader is at her best with varied activities, autonomy, and projects that produce tangible results. When resistant, the Leader style tries to run the show. She's easily frustrated and sometimes argumentative when the big picture doesn't look the way she wants it to be.

BOB: The Leader style is a camera lens that's usually set on extreme wide angle, so details look fuzzy. Help the Leader zoom in a bit – not all the way to telephoto – but, enough to focus on what is working well right now. Do this by asking questions that break an issue down into smaller components. Once the Leader has identified all of the parts, ask her to pick one component to focus on and improve. Turn that piece of the project into a game, and put the Leader in charge of winning it.

I'm the new manager of an engineering team. Mark reports to me and is the senior contributor on the team. We refer to his character as "Leader," not because he's the boss, but because it's his style type. Let's see if I'm able to influence his behavior.

CONVERSATION WITH A RESISTANT LEADER

BOSS: I want you to develop a prototype of an atom splitter.

LEADER: That won't work. We tried that before you got here.

BOSS: Okay, what will work? (Notices his head pull back in surprise)

LEADER: Nothing really. We should shift our efforts to another product.

BOSS: That's not an option. What are the reasons it didn't work before?

LEADER: Not enough time or money. The company has to fully fund prototype development and stop trying to do everything on the cheap.

BOSS: How much time and money?

LEADER: Three months and $750K.

BOSS: How could you cut that in half?

LEADER: That would be hard to do.

BOSS: How could you get a good enough prototype in six weeks with $375K so that we could recoup our investment in six months and then continue product development?

LEADER: It'll take me some time to rough out a proposal.

BOSS: I'm looking forward to seeing your ideas. When can we discuss it?

LEADER: I'll have some numbers for you in two weeks.

At the end of their role-play, the pair summarized tips for communicating when a Leader type is resistant:

- Acknowledge her leadership strengths: "Your project vision inspired the team."

- Ask Open-Ended "What" questions that highlight the benefits of an approach: "What could go well if we went with Jim's plan?"

- Ask "Who" questions that point out the impact on others: "Who will be satisfied with this option?"

- Ask "How" questions that elicit ideas and a leadership mindset: "How can you make the design so unique that the industry will notice?"

- Consciously Pause and listen to her innovative ideas, and then ask her to weigh the pros and cons of each: "You've got an intriguing proposal. What aspects of it do you think will be supported and rejected?"

- Use Laser Messages to set concise performance expectations for learning to break large projects into specific deliverables and for developing team skills like listening and showing appreciation of other's opinions, feelings, and contributions: "During our next team meeting, I want to hear you acknowledge at least one person for a specific accomplishment."

SLOW DOWN THE SOCIALIZER

Ravi and Suzie were next. They described the Socializer as a people-oriented extrovert. A Socializer is at her best when solving problems, motivating others, and negotiating conflicts. When resistant, the Socializing style may distract the conversation by changing the subject, making a joke, or rationalizing why assignments are late.

> RAVI: Suzie is a Socializer and my administrative assistant. Notice in the following conversation how the Socializer's mind resists focusing on the conversation topic. Instead, it expands to include everybody and everything. The Socializer's mind is like a kid in a candy store; it points at everything and wants all of it right now! I'll stay mindful of her communication and my internal reactions as I use Laser Messages, Open-Ended Questions, and surfacing what is happening in the conversation to slow down the social mind and *focus* it on one point: my performance expectation.

CONVERSATION WITH A RESISTANT SOCIALIZER

BOSS: We still don't have new furniture for the lobby.

SOCIALIZER: I haven't had time to order it. This move is slamming me. People are complaining to me about their offices, and I haven't gotten any help setting up the filing or unpacking these boxes. And, my daughter and her husband are coming with the kids this weekend. Did I show you the pictures she sent last week? The twins are adorable. Look at these. Aren't they precious? We're having a cookout on Saturday if you want to come by. Just burgers. Oh, you don't eat meat. Well, there will be plenty of potato salad. Oh that reminds me I need to...

BOSS (Using **Feet & Seat** to stay calm): Excuse me. I'm sorry to interrupt. Thanks for the invitation. I'm sorry I won't be able to make it. Let's shift back to the move. You've done a great job handling so many aspects of it. How can you make the furniture order a priority today?

SOCIALIZER: I don't see how I can get to it. I've got to get the invitations for the Open House in the mail today. It's only two weeks away. Jill is out sick, so I'll have to cover the phones. And, I have a dentist appointment this afternoon, so I'm leaving at three o'clock, which reminds me, I could stop at the store on the way to the dentist to pick up...

BOSS (Surfacing what is happening in the present moment): Excuse me. You're really good at noticing details. What do you notice is happening in our conversation right now?

SOCIALIZER: What do you mean? We're talking. That's all I notice.

BOSS: Right, we're talking. What are you talking about?

SOCIALIZER: Everything I need to get done today, and by the way, I'm getting farther behind, because this conversation is taking so long.

BOSS (Reflecting her feelings and refocusing on expectation): I can tell you're frustrated. And, what am I talking about?

SOCIALIZER: The furniture for the lobby. I don't have time to deal with that today.

BOSS (Asking the **Open-Ended Question**): What are three important reasons for ordering the furniture this morning?

SOCIALIZER: We need it before the Open House, it'll make all of us feel more at home here, and I'll get it off of my to-do list.

BOSS: Thanks. Those are three good reasons. How long will it take you to order it?

SOCIALIZER: I don't have time. I'm slammed.

BOSS (*Noticing* the other person's upset, taking a *breath*, and *allowing* her to be uncomfortable without taking it on himself): I hear that you're feeling overwhelmed. I'm just curious how long it would take to order it if you had the time?

SOCIALIZER: Since we've already picked it out, I guess it might take 30 minutes to make the call. But I have to cover the phones, so it'll be a big pain to keep putting the salesperson on hold when a call comes in, which reminds me I have to order a cake for the cookout. What kind of icing do people like best on chocolate cake, vanilla or chocolate?

BOSS (**Facts & Feelings** about self, Refocusing, and **Open-Ended Question**): I'm feeling frustrated that we haven't finished this conversation yet. Let's get back to the furniture. Who could you ask to cover the phones for an hour just in case you need that much time?

SOCIALIZER: I guess Brad could do it.

BOSS: Good idea. Tell him that I approved you asking for his help on this. Ordering the furniture is your top priority this morning. When you're finished, email me the delivery date.

When they finished the role-play, Suzie recapped the key points.

SUZIE: After hearing that scenario, you might be thinking, "I don't have time to tell people what their priorities are every day or to find a work-around for them." You're right. Your direct reports should be able to prioritize their to-do lists in a way that matches your expectations and meets their needs. Unfortunately, not everyone knows how to do that. The Socializer in this scenario has developmental gaps around prioritization and follow-through. Instead of ignoring these gaps or getting angry about them, Ravi might need to address my behavior in future conversations so that it doesn't continue to be an issue.

RAVI: That's right. If Suzie continues to ramble off topic, I'll ask her to *notice* her behavioral pattern of changing the subject particularly to personal issues. Together, we would brainstorm ways to help her concentrate on the conversation topic without bringing up extraneous subjects. Gently and consistently bringing her mind back to the topic is the third Influence Step of *focus*.

Suzie summarized tools for communicating with a resistant Socializer:

• Acknowledge her contributions with fun, authentic Laser praise: "You must have super powers. Thank you for running such a flawless event."

• Ask Open-Ended "How" questions to develop practical procedures: "How could you streamline the hiring process so that it only takes six weeks?"

• Ask "Who" questions to create professional and social group activities: "Who should we invite to this networking event?"

• Ask "When" questions to get a commitment on a specific deadline: "You've got a lot on your plate. When are you absolutely positive you can deliver this spread sheet?"

• Consciously Pause and listen to her gut instincts about people and projects, and then ask her to supply backup data: "I hear that you're worried about adding Linda to the team. What are her specific behaviors that concern you most? How have you tried to address those with her in the past?"

• Set performance expectations for providing results on time, controlling emotions, and listening more: "You're angry about the strategic plan. Right? I'd like to hear you calmly explain suggestions for improving it."

HELP THE THINKER ZOOM OUT

Randall and Jasmine asked to present next.

RANDALL: I had to laugh when Jasmine told me that we got the Thinker style. I told her I wouldn't need a script, because I overdo that style every day. The Thinker is a task-oriented introvert. A Thinker is happiest with detailed tasks, logical routines, and limited social interaction. When resistant, a Thinker may distract the conversation by complaining about not having adequate resources to do a thorough job or about team members who don't follow procedures.

JASMINE: While the Leader style that Mark portrayed has a mind that expands to the big picture, the Thinker's mind often contracts to focus on a limited set of minute details just like a camera lens set on extreme close-up. Since this style fears making mistakes, a Thinker can be a perfectionist or slow decision maker. I'll show you how to use the Influence Tools to gently open the Thinker's lens. Slowly expand this style's awareness from one small slice of flat terrain to include the whole divergent landscape and all the interesting people in it.

RANDALL: Jasmine is the CEO of a large company that is trying to develop an international market. I'm the CFO, and a Thinker style. Notice how she uses the Influence Steps – **Speak - Observe - Focus** – throughout the conversation.

CONVERSATION WITH A RESISTANT THINKER

CEO (*Speaks* a laser observation): You missed another Senior Management Team (SMT) meeting today.

THINKER: I had to finish editing the Annual Report.

CEO (Calmly *observes* resistance and *speaks* her expectation): You're the Chief Financial Officer. I need you at every meeting.

THINKER (Exasperated): The report was about to go to print, and the font in half of the tables was 11 instead of 10. Someone needed to catch those errors.

CEO (*Focuses* on expectation): You've missed three SMT meetings in a row.

THINKER (grimaces and silently stares at the wall)

CEO (**Facts & Feelings, Open-Ended Question**): I know that you generally dislike meetings, but you've always made it to SMTs. What changed?

THINKER (grits teeth): I'm busy. I'm trying to run this department with two key positions open and no viable candidates in sight. And, if the Marketing Division would try submitting accurate travel reports just once, then maybe this company wouldn't be going to pot.

CEO (**Feelings**): You sound angry.

THINKER: The corporation has procedures for one reason: consistency. The Marketing Division seems to think the travel policy doesn't apply to them. They think I'm in here printing money, so they can send their employees all over the world supposedly developing business. I haven't seen any new contracts yet.

CEO (*Observes* CFO's anger and doesn't take it on): That's what I need you to say in the SMT meeting.

THINKER: I've tried, and she just rolls her eyes and walks out laughing.

CEO (Expanding the lens with **Open-Ended Question**): You're right that we need to hold everyone accountable for the travel policy. At the same time, what's the broader issue here?

THINKER: The broader issue? Marketing doesn't follow any company policies?!

CEO (Expanding the lens): How could you show leadership on this issue?

THINKER: What do you mean?

CEO (Narrowing the lens): You're the go-to person on financials. What would you do if one of your managers wasn't following the travel policy?

THINKER: I'd talk with the person. Find out what was going on. There'd be a good explanation, because my people never break a policy unless there's a very, very, very good reason.

CEO: How could you give Rachel in Marketing the same benefit of the doubt?

THINKER (long pause): I guess I could drop by her office and ask her what's going on. Then I wouldn't have to bring it up in front of everyone in our next SMT.

CEO (*Focus*): When can you do that?

THINKER: I was headed to the third floor anyway. I'll email her to see if she's got a few minutes to talk. I'm not hopeful it will help though.

CEO: Keep an open mind. Let me know how it goes. If you two don't resolve this, send the issue to Jerry for the next SMT agenda.

I want you to take the lead on that discussion. We might need to tighten accountability or adjust the policy.

After their role-play, Jasmine compared the Thinker and Leader styles. Most people have trained their minds to work in a certain way most of the time. Without getting too stereotypical, it might be safe to generalize and say that accountants usually focus on details, while CEOs tend to see the big picture. The good news is that everyone's mind is relatively elastic and trainable. Stay calm and mindful of their comments; they will tell you how large or small their lens is. You can teach a Thinker or a Leader style how to expand and contract her camera lens on her own. Then, she can move back and forth from the details to the big picture when necessary and without much assistance from you. To summarize, Randall shared a list of tips for communicating with a resistant Thinker:

• Reassure her that she is doing what is expected of her: "Nice job on the financial reports; they were thorough and easy to read."

• Ask Open-Ended "What" questions to elicit her concerns and ideas: "What could we do to improve customer service response time?"

• Ask "Who" questions to determine team players she respects: "Who impressed you the most on this new product roll-out?"

• Ask "When" questions to determine a deadline that won't let her get too bogged down in details: "I need your help next week on another project. When is the earliest possible time you can finish a rough draft of this model, so that you can shift your focus?"

• Consciously Pause and listen to her concerns about new initiatives, and then ask what resources she has for adapting to change. "It sounds like you're concerned about having to learn a new software program. When you had to learn a new system in the past, what steps did you take that helped you quickly get up to speed on it?"

• Set Laser performance expectations for her to take risks rather than stick with a routine, be less critical of others, and build relationships with other team members: "I know that you prefer to work on your own, but we're asking everyone to volunteer for one committee. Which one interests you the most?"

SPEED UP THE RELATER

JANICE: We saved the best for last.

JUAN: This is the hardest case study, Suzanne. The reason I said earlier that Janice's character is tough to influence is because she's my boss.

SUZANNE: It's challenging to hold the person above you account-able, Juan. However, there are neutral ways to address a superior without being bossy or out of line. And, being honest with the boss is an important developmental step for a mindful leader. It's important to cultivate a collegial rapport. And, frankly, upper management is looking for strong folks – not "Yes" people – to promote.

Janice described their findings. The Relater is a people-oriented introvert who is at her best with clearly defined goals and roles, the chance to help team members, and support from people or processes. When resistant, a Relater may be slow, unmotivated, and fearful of expressing her concerns particularly if it involves people.

Juan explained that the Socializer's expansiveness and the Thinker's contraction are relatively easy to spot. But, the Relater's resistance is more subtle. He encouraged the group to notice the subtle ways in which the Relater tends to go along to get along. While a Socializer wants everything in the candy store, the Relater stands back and lets everyone else go first by saying, "It's okay. I don't care. I'll take whatever's left."

The Relater doesn't want to rock the boat, because she's very sensitive to feed-back. Be mindful of the Relater's verbal and nonverbal mechanisms that communicate, "I'm easily hurt. Don't hurt me, too." These mechanisms include changing the subject, avoiding confrontation, and even crying. As a result, you might be more hesitant to point out her performance gaps. When communicating with a Relater, *notice* if you mirror her fear by avoiding challenging issues.

Mark interjected that this was his problem with Dana's crying. In order to break his ineffective pattern with her, he had to have high intrapersonal attunement, so that he could *notice* when he become passive as soon as she began to cry.

Janice said that their role-play shows how a manager – played by Juan – deals with his Relater boss' resistance to making a client phone call. A Relater Boss can be tricky. She asked the group to *notice* how she tries to push the responsibility back on Juan by putting herself down. Self-critical comments are an attempt to win his sympathy, so that he will let her off the hook.

CONVERSATION WITH A RESISTANT RELATER BOSS

MANAGER: I wanted to check in with you about the Jones project. You said you would contact the client about our offer.

RELATER BOSS: I haven't heard back from him since you sent that email.

MANAGER (Calmly *speaks* the facts): I know. I sent that email two weeks ago. That's why when we talked last week you offered to follow up with a phone call to him.

RELATER BOSS: I've been so busy working on my Social Marketing presentation for the national conference next week. What time are you flying in? I really hope you can have dinner with Joe and me.

MANAGER (*Refocuses* on expectation): Thanks. My flight gets in at six o'clock, so I'm pretty sure I'll be able to meet you two. Oh, back to the Jones project. It would be a big piece of business for us.

RELATER BOSS: I know, I know. I'm so awful for not calling. It's just such an honor to be asked to present at this conference. And, I've been trying to be available for Mary whenever she needs to talk about her father's death. She's having trouble concentrating on her work.

MANAGER (**Facts & Feelings** of boss and self): You're right to be concerned about the conference and Mary; they're important issues. However, I'm nervous about the Jones proposal. When we talked about it last week, you felt that you were the best person to follow-up, and I agreed. I really appreciated your offer to help on this and would like to support you in making that call in any way I can.

RELATER BOSS: You're right. I'm awful. I'll call him today.

MANAGER (*Observes* and surfaces the attempted deflection): I didn't say you're awful.

RELATER BOSS: But, you're thinking it.

MANAGER: How do you know that?

RELATER BOSS: Because you're angry.

MANAGER: What am I doing or saying that makes you think I'm angry?

RELATER BOSS: I don't know. I just know you're angry.

MANAGER (Replying, "No, I'm not angry" might end the conversation. Instead, an **Open-Ended Question** gets information): I appreciate your honesty about this, because I want feedback about how I come across to people. This might be hard to do, but I'd like to know what I look like right now that makes you think I'm angry, so that I can change it. I don't want my direct reports to think I'm mad when I'm not. How does my face or body look right now that makes you think I'm angry?

RELATER BOSS: I don't know what you mean.

MANAGER: What do angry people look like?

RELATER BOSS: Tense. Hot. Like they're going to explode.

MANAGER: I agree. Where have you seen those signs in me since we started this conversation, for example, in my facial expressions or how I'm talking?

RELATER BOSS: Well, right now I don't see them. You look relaxed.

MANAGER: Thanks. I feel pretty calm. I don't feel angry or upset about the Jones thing at all.

RELATER BOSS: But even if you don't look angry, you must be fuming inside, and you're just not showing it. You must be thinking that I'm lazy for not calling Jones.

MANAGER (Calmly *speaks* **Facts**): It sounds like you're making up what I'm thinking.

RELATER BOSS: I guess I am. I never thought about it that way. But, aren't you having those thoughts?

MANAGER: Honestly, I'm not. I'm having thoughts like: "What's preventing you from making this call? How can I help you be a success with this challenging client?" Those are my thoughts.

RELATER BOSS: That's all?

MANAGER: Yes.

RELATER BOSS: I guess I was imagining all of that. Sorry about that. I promised to help you out by making a call, but let's face it, that guy is tough.

MANAGER: I agree. He's not an easy sell, and he's hard to read. Frankly, I do the same thing, wondering what people are thinking. Like Jones. When he didn't respond to my email, I *noticed* I was guessing his thoughts. I imagined him thinking, "Their prices are inflated. The service options are limited. I'm not going to respond to this email, and if he calls, I won't talk to him." Stuff like that. If I'm thinking that's what he's thinking, of course I wouldn't want to call him.

RELATER BOSS: I was thinking about him along the same lines. It's a waste of time to make up people's thoughts, isn't it? We have no idea what he's thinking. Maybe he didn't respond to your email because he's on vacation. What do you think we should do?

MANAGER: He's a social type. Maybe we should wait to talk with him face to face at the conference. Take him out for dinner, and ask him what he's thinking.

RELATER BOSS: Good idea. Hey, thanks for pointing this out about my thoughts. In the future, let's try to catch ourselves and each other if it seems like we're imagining the worst.

MANAGER: Sounds good. So, who should take the next step about Jones?

RELATER BOSS: Stay there. I'm going to call him right now to schedule dinner…

Janice asked for feedback about their role-play and wondered if it would feel scary or insubordinate to talk with Karen this way. The group laughed.

KAREN: I hope not. Imagine if this manager had let his boss rationalize her behavior. That sets up a negative pattern of letting a boss default on a promise by making up an excuse and then calling him or herself a bad person. Don't let anyone, including me, get away with such a superficial defense. Janice wasn't overbooked or lazy; she was afraid. If Juan let her get away with that, she'd use the excuse in the future. And, Juan would never be able to help her identify and overcome her performance gap – fear of a challenging phone call. I hope each of you would feel comfortable pointing something like this out to me. I want you to.

Juan summarized the tools he used. In addition to self-disclosure, each of the Influence Tools can help you manage up. Deliver a Laser Message of what you want: "The Jones project would be a big win for us." Ask Open-Ended Questions that show your willingness to help: "How can I help you get this done?" Use Facts & Feelings to reflect your boss' experience: "This guy can be intimidating, can't he?" If those tools don't work and you *notice* that you're getting irritated with your boss, use BEER to add an effect and request: "When you say you'll call a client for me but don't (behavior), the project gets stalled (effect), and I feel confused (emotion) about my role. Would you be willing to explain the biggest barrier to making the call? (request)" Remember to deliver one piece of the formula at a time with Pauses in between to let her respond if she wants to. Then, he shared a list of tips for communicating with a resistant Relater:

• Express appreciation for her loyalty and dependability: "You're our safety net. Thank you for keeping us updated on new federal regulations."

• Ask Open-Ended "How" questions to elicit ideas on how procedures and systems could be improved: "How can I do a better job updating you on my team's progress?"

• Ask "Who" questions to elicit who she enjoys working with: "Who would you like to work with on the program's beta test?"

• Ask "What" questions to encourage new areas of responsibility: "What new project could you take on that would help you develop a different skill set?"

• Consciously Pause and listen to how she agrees with everything you say, and then ask what is missing or what she slightly disagrees with: "What did I leave out of that task description that you're wondering about?"

• Set performance expectations so that she uses more direct communication, increases the pace to accomplish goals, and takes more initiative: "I really appreciate that your error rate on entering client data is so low. What could you do to increase your speed while maintaining your accuracy?"

SUMMARIZING THE RETREAT

After the last presentation, I thanked everyone for their work on the case studies and the rousing role-plays. We reviewed the Influence Tools, and I gave people time to develop an individual action plan for applying the tools in their work.

> SUZANNE: For your confidential coaching conversation with me tomorrow, please bring a specific issue or case that you want to discuss. To finish up, who would like to share what their most valuable take away was from the retreat today?

MARK: Less is more.

BOB: The pause that refreshes.

JUAN: Talking about feelings isn't therapy. It might shift a conversation to a more honest level. And, it could uncover the real barriers that haven't been addressed and are blocking a solution.

SUZIE: Who, what, when, where, and how are my new best friends.

JANICE: I like **Speak - Observe - Focus**. No matter what's happening in a conversation, I'll mindfully keep repeating those steps to concentrate the other person's mind on my expectation.

SUZANNE: Thank you, all. I've thoroughly enjoyed working with you today and look forward to coaching with you tomorrow. Please leave your evaluation forms on the large table. And, you'll see some Mind to Lead CDs on the table. There's one for each of you. They have several guided mindfulness exercises for developing a focused, calm mind on the job.

KAREN: Suzanne, thank you very much for today. I'm excited that our management team had this chance to learn and practice the Influence Tools with you. And, we look forward to bringing you back.

As I was packing my brief case, Karen walked up to say thanks.

KAREN: That was outstanding, Suzanne. I was thrilled by everyone's participation and even the challenging questions. Though it wasn't a team building retreat, per se, I feel the team grew closer and was more honest today than ever before. Very exciting. You and I are having lunch tomorrow, right?

SUZANNE: Yes. I'm looking forward to it. I'll bring a summary of the evaluation forms, so that we can debrief the retreat. Karen, I appreciate your support today. It was a pleasure to work with everyone. You've built a strong, successful team.

POST SCRIPT

In the coaching sessions the next day, each manager had the chance to ask follow up questions about the retreat. We also refined their action plans for using the tools and coached around a challenging situation.

At the end of lunch, Karen said she was headed to an offsite meeting for the afternoon. "I'm looking forward to our regular call next week, Suzanne."

"Me, too, Karen," I replied.

Karen and I continued coaching for two more years. Despite challenges in the economy and to their business, she grew more calm and confident as a leader, and continued to increase her influence both within her Division and across the company. I hope her story and the following stories in Part Three of nine other mindful leaders I've coached will inspire you as a leader.

CONCEPTS

- Power isn't about control; it's about responsibility. It's your responsibility to influence people in a way that achieves the organization's goals.

- Use the Influence Steps – **SPEAK - OBSERVE - FOCUS** – to clearly communicate your intention, first, to yourself and then to the other person.

- Select appropriate Influence Tools based on whether the situation calls for a Tell or Ask approach. You might move back and forth between these two strategies by using **Laser Messages, Facts & Feelings, Open-Ended Questions**, and/or **BEER**.

- Flex your style. When you first meet resistance, identify in your mind the other person's style as Leader, Socializer, Thinker, or Relater. Adapt your communication approach to reduce her specific style of resistant and to assure that she completes the task.

In **Part Three,** you'll see how nine mindful leaders adapted their communication style to reduce resistance in another person.

PART THREE

MERGING THE MINDSETS FOR LEADERSHIP SUCCESS: MANAGING UP, DOWN, AND ACROSS

This section describes nine case studies of how my clients used combinations of Mindfulness, Exploration, and Influence to develop Calm, Confident Power and be more effective. Each case study blends tools described in previous sections of the book and applies them to varied situations. Each case is presented in an easy-to-read format, using this 5-S Coaching Model:

1. **SITUATION**: Introduces the people and issues.

2. **SYMPTOMS**: Describes the pain each person was experiencing.

3. **SOURCE**: Identifies the unproductive, reactive pattern that each person was repeating and may include their **Reporter's** relative skill level at mindfulness.

4. **SOLUTION**: Outlines the action that the mindful leader took to reduce the painful symptoms including which Mind to Lead processes or tools were used.

5. **SHIFT**: Summarizes the change in a pattern that each person experienced to become a Calm, Confident and Powerful Leader

Chapter 7 covers managing up (boss), **Chapter 8** deals with managing down (direct report), and **Chapter 9** is about managing across (colleague).

CHAPTER 7

MANAGING UP:
SETTING BOUNDARIES WITH YOUR BOSS

I hope that you have a productive relationship with your boss. For mindful leaders who don't, it's normal to feel powerless at influencing that relationship. The three case studies in this chapter show how a brave, clever leader can impact the person above him:

Case Study 1: My boss controls my career.

Case Study 2: My boss doesn't trust me.

Case Study 3: I don't respect my boss.

CASE STUDY 1: MY BOSS CONTROLS MY CAREER

SITUATION: Mel was a 49-year-old lawyer who ran the advocacy department at a non-governmental organization in Washington, DC; he managed 12 people. Since taking the job two years earlier, he'd made considerable improvements in the department. All employees were now full contributors, and error rates in the massive databases they managed were almost zero. While he wanted to keep making progress with this team, Mel was already a bit bored with his job and interested in moving up in management. Even though he believed that his boss, Ada, didn't appreciate his work and might even be happy to get rid of him, Mel also feared that she would block his attempts to be promoted out of the department.

SYMPTOMS: Mel had many painful thoughts about his boss: "Ada doesn't trust me, Ada would block a promotion for me, and I'll have to hide that I'm applying for other positions." His thinking had immobilized him, and he was afraid to ask for Ada's help.

SOURCE: Mel let other people influence how he thought about and what he did about his career. Even though he had never practiced mindfulness, he was able to very quickly discover his **Reporter**, *notice* his negative beliefs about Ada, and see how they were immobilizing his job search.

SOLUTION: In our first coaching conversation, Mel used Exploration to *listen* to and *inquire* into his thoughts about Ada. He realized that thoughts like, "Ada won't let me move up" and "I'm not valued at all" were unproven and preventing him from taking action. After exploring his thoughts about Ada, Mel felt less judgmental about her and more confident about asking for her help.

At the end of our first call, he committed to talking with Ada. However, in our next conversation two weeks later, he said he'd been too busy and hadn't followed through. I told him that it's normal to feel intimidated about talking with his boss particularly if he didn't fully respect her and guessed his feelings were reciprocated.

As we talked more, Mel admitted deeper concerns about Ada controlling his career. He was afraid that she could be trying to sabotage him. When I asked for evidence, Mel had no proof that Ada was speaking poorly about him to other people.

After we did The Work© on his strongest concern, "I need to know what she says about me," Mel realized that he had no idea what Ada was thinking or doing, and it didn't matter. He *affirmed* this insight: "It's important for me to stay confident and in my own business." He was ready to stop giving his power away and stop imagining that Ada was plotting against him.

To move our conversation forward, I asked, "What gifts have you received from Ada?" He replied, "She's a tremendous gift, because she lets me look at myself and see the qualities that I don't want to display as a leader. She also leaves me alone to manage my department, and unless I messed up really badly, she can't hurt my reputation."

That's the confidence I wanted Mel to have before he talked with Ada. He wrote a clear request he would make of her, and he understood that it was up to her if she wanted to help him or not. If she didn't want to help, he could find other allies.

We also talked about how he could use **Feet & Seat** before and during the conversation. This tool would help him stay calm and focused on his goal for their meeting.

In our next call, Mel was proud of a very successful conversation he had with Ada. "I was in control. I was able to be myself and express my feelings without being reactive or overly personal. I really stuck to my agenda by using the Influence Process (**Speak - Observe - Focus**). I told her what I wanted and asked how she could help. I told her I was interested in two different management positions, and she said, 'Good. Apply for both of them, and I'll make some phone calls to get you connected with people who can get you more information about the jobs.'" Simply by telling the truth to Ada, Mel took control of his career.

A couple weeks later in another coaching call, Mel said that he *noticed* he was again overreacting to Ada. He was having more upsetting thoughts about her like, "She's out to get me. She doesn't trust me." He said that he explored and neutralized those thoughts on his own. "I wanted to go into my next conversation with her and completely tell the truth of what was going on in my own mind." He sounded very confident. We made a plan so that he could discuss his true concerns with Ada.

In our next call, Mel described what he had said in their most recent meeting, "Ada, sometimes when I read your emails, I completely overreact. Instead of focusing on the content of the message, I start to think, 'Okay, here's what Ada's really thinking.' And, I always imagine it's really negative. Then, I realize that I'm just making up what you're thinking." Mel said that he **Paused**, looked at Ada, and continued, "I'm wondering if you ever have a reaction to my emails like that. And, I'm wondering if you want to talk about how we could work together better."

I was really impressed. I took a deep breath and asked what happened next.

"Ada looked at me, and said, 'I agree with you.'"

Wow! A major breakthrough.

"It was the best discussion I've ever had with a boss. It completely changed the dynamic between us, and I was so relieved to get these feelings off my chest. I didn't go into the conversation focusing on how she might respond or thinking, 'Oh, she's going to do this,' or 'What if she does that?' I focused my mind on my business. It was amazing. I wasn't nervous at all."

SHIFT: Though he was initially passive and intimidated by Ada, Mel created a completely new relationship with his boss and became a more Confident Leader simply by staying calm, telling the truth, and asking if she wanted to help him. Though Mel didn't get either of the positions, he's more satisfied with his job and comfortable working with Ada.

CASE STUDY 2: MY BOSS DOESN'T TRUST ME

SITUATION: Julie was a 33-year-old mom-to-be who ran an internal security program in a large manufacturing company; she had five employees. Julie thought her boss, Renee, did a pretty good job. Though, sometimes Renee made decisions that ignored Julie and her team.

SYMPTOMS: They'd gotten along all right until recently when Renee got a new director-level boss. Julie felt that Renee's new boss was micromanaging Renee and pushing her to control Julie and the other managers more. Julie was irritated by Renee's new behavior.

When I asked what thoughts Julie was having about Renee, Julie's **Reporter** was quick to respond, "You haven't empowered me to do my job. You won't let me take action without your approval."

SOURCE: Julie *noticed* that this pattern of thoughts wasn't just about Renee. In reflecting on her prior work history, she reported that she felt upset and threatened when anyone told her or even suggested what she should do.

SOLUTION: After I described the four style types (Figure 7.1) to Julie, we agreed that she was a combination Thinker-Socializer. Details and connecting with people were important to her. Renee's primary style, on the other hand, was Leading; she focused on results. As we talked about the different styles, Julie had a sudden "ah-ha!" "Oh, this reminds me. Renee is really interested in style types. She took a class on styles recently and told me about it."

TABLE 7.1 STYLE TYPES

STYLES	TASK FOCUS	PEOPLE FOCUS
Extrovert	Leading	Socializing
Introvert	Thinking	Relating

When I asked if discussing their styles was a good way to bring up her upset about Renee's recent behavior change, Julie liked the idea. "I'm just going to bring it up in a conversation and ask permission to talk about styles a little bit more. Since she's already mentioned it, I feel comfortable talking about how our styles are alike and different."

Renee was happy that Julie had remembered the topic, and she was open to discussing it. Feeling her **Feet & Seat** and taking a few slow breaths, Julie pulled out a copy of the Styles table and asked, "Which style are you, and which style do you think I am?" The conversation continued as Julie asked, "How do you think we're similar, and how do you think we're different?"

Notice that Julie wasn't confrontational; she didn't blame Renee by saying, "I don't like it when you try to control me," or "I don't think you trust me, because you talk down to me like I'm your daughter." Instead, she was curious about Renee's point of view, and asked **Open-Ended Questions** like, "How do you think our different styles impact how we each approach leadership?"

Julie followed the Influence Process when, first, she *spoke* about a theoretical model to jump-start what could have been a difficult conversation with her boss. Then, she *observed* that Renee was enjoying the conversation; they were learning and laughing about their similarities and differences. That's when Julie *focused* the conversation on her goal by asking permission to shift to solutions.

JULIE: Can we talk about how we could work together even better?

RENEE: Sure, what do you have in mind?

JULIE: My coach taught me a tool called, More Of/Less Of for making requests of someone. We would each request what we want more of or less of.

RENEE: Okay, I'd be willing to hear a request.

JULIE: (Taking a deep inhale and exhale) Here goes. Would you be willing to acknowledge my accomplishments more when we meet with senior management?

RENEE: Sure, I can do that. What else?

JULIE: I'd like less frequent requests on all the details of my team meetings.

RENEE: That won't be as easy to do, Julie. My new boss, Greg, is pushing for a lot more information than Roger did. Let me try a More of/Less of on you. I want you to send me a more detailed report of your weekly team meetings, so that I have the information on a routine basis and won't have to ask you about it. Let's negotiate how much detail should go into that report.

JULIE: Okay, that's fair.

SHIFT: Instead of giving Julie's report for her at the next senior management meeting, Renee asked Julie to present. Then, Renee commented that Julie was always well-prepared and reliable. Julie used **Notice - Breathe - Allow** to feel in her body how wonderful it was to hear Renee's acknowledgement. Over time, Renee set firmer boundaries with her boss, Greg. Over time, Greg trusted Renee more and asked her for fewer details. As a result, Renee let up on micromanaging Julie and her other managers.

These behavioral shifts originated from a shift in Julie's thinking. Once Julie realized that she could try talking honestly with her boss, she calmly brought up the issue of styles and made a request of Renee. This changed their professional relationship, and Renee also began making more direct requests of Julie and of her own boss.

Another shift occurred when Julie started giving more specific, positive feedback to Renee. You might think that "thank you" is enough for your boss. However, acknowledging specific behaviors that you want your boss to repeat is an ethical way to exert influence and be a more Powerful Leader. For example, Julie used the **BEER** formula: "Renee, when you give me the authority to learn how to post my temporary job position on my own (behavior), I feel happy (emotion), because you're empowering me to learn new management tasks (effect) even when I'm preparing to go on maternity leave. Please keep it up (request)." Like everyone else, bosses enjoy hearing what they're doing right.

CASE STUDY 3: I DON'T RESPECT MY BOSS

SITUATION: Ann was the 39-year-old leader of a large import/export company's multi-national shipping and receiving division. She had a $5 million budget and 22 direct reports.

When I asked Ann in our initial coaching session to describe her boss, she said, "Nabil is incompetent. He doesn't know operational requirements. And, it's extremely frustrating that nothing I do is ever good enough for him."

SYMPTOMS: Ann was familiar with the style types. "I can't be myself with Nabil. I have to turn off my natural Socializing style, and put on a fake Leading style, so that I act like him. I'm very uncomfortable working for him. I'm self-assured with my employees, but lose my confidence with him."

Ann was angry, because Nabil asked all of his division heads to have a monthly meeting with each of their direct reports. Ann felt this was unnecessary. She did a lot of management by walking around, was in touch with what her employees were doing, and didn't want to have 22 individual meetings every month. But, Nabil continued to push her on it.

Ann felt that she was in a corner. "I've got two options: I can do what Nabil wants and not feel good about it. Or, I can do what I want, feel good about myself, but feel badly that I probably won't get a good raise and that I'm sabotaging my career."

SOURCE: To help Ann relax, be less reactive, and uncover the broader issue, I asked her to take a few moments with the Mindfulness Process to **Notice - Breathe - Allow** her reactions to previous bosses. As we talked, she became aware of an unproductive pattern with past supervisors. If a boss wasn't like her, Ann would lose her cool and fight back instead of trying to get to know him or her. Ann recognized that repeatedly over her career, it hadn't worked to fight or ignore bosses who were different from her. Her "Ah-ha!" from our first call was a mindset shift from resistant to curious: "I want to understand Nabil better and what he really needs from me as my boss."

SOLUTION: For our next call, I asked Ann to complete The Work's© worksheet called Judge Your Neighbor©, so that we could investigate her thoughts about Nabil. Ann had a variety of thoughts about him including: "Nabil wants everyone to manage like he does." "Nabil is wound up; he runs around causing more problems than he fixes." "I'm really grateful that Nabil gave me a shot at this management position." Ann could see her internal conflict about Nabil. A mixture of gratitude and dislike for a person is very common and often a key reason for a person's frustration and inaction.

I encouraged Ann to use **Mindful Breathing** to relax while we investigated the thought, "Nabil wants everyone to manage like he does." Ann admitted that she didn't know Nabil's thoughts or wishes. She also realized that because this thought upset her, she didn't listen to or appreciate his leadership.

Ann's biggest insight came from turning the thought around to, "I want everyone to manage like I do, particularly Nabil." Though Ann had always accepted her employees' varied styles, she expected her boss to act just like her. It's common for leaders to want to see their own style reflected in their boss. A mirrored style affirms the leader, and makes her feel safe. Unfortunately, it's a numbers game, and you've only got a one in four chance of matching your boss' style. Ann could see how unrealistic and unfair her expectations of Nabil were.

Ann and I talked more about Nabil's Leading style. He had a very strong **Tell** approach, while she used a more congenial, **Ask** style. Ann decided to try **Flexing Her Style** -- a Powerful Leader tool -- by using Nabil's communication approach on him.

At their next meeting, Ann was equal parts nervous and excited, which she labeled internally using the Mindful Feeling tool. That helped her calm down, so that right off the bat, she delivered a strong **Laser Message**, "I don't want to hold regular employee meetings." His reply? "That's fine."

Ann was stunned. They had argued about employee meetings for weeks. But now, he didn't need to talk about them or hear her reasoning. Could it be that easy? It was like some weird Star Trek episode. To neutralize Nabil, all she had to do was act like him. And, she didn't have to act like him all the time; short **Tell** injections were enough. Ann was learning that *listening* to and investigating her unpleasant thoughts allowed her to neutralize the stressful beliefs, *affirm* what was really true, and come across as a completely Confident Leader with Nabil. When she changed, Nabil changed a bit, too.

IT'S ALL ABOUT ME

Ann was riding high after her first successful conversation with Nabil. Unfortunately, she didn't realize that even though she had changed a great deal, Nabil hadn't changed that much. He was still Nabil, and she still felt reactive and disappointed. On our next call, Ann began to understand how much she suffered about this. Her mind continued to want the "perfect boss" version of Nabil – who would be just like Ann.

I asked, "How can you be the leader that you want Nabil to be?" This helped Ann shift from complaining about and confronting Nabil to recognizing her own developmental needs. She wanted to be more direct, consistent, and supportive with her employees. As she saw that she could be the mindful leader that she wanted Nabil to be, she let go more of needing him to be different than he was.

As Ann used the Tell technique more with Nabil, their relationship shifted and her confidence increased. She was boldly going where no man had gone before. Nevertheless, there were still some unexplored, strange new worlds. So, I continued to ask what else was bugging her. On our next call, she said she was disappointed that Nabil never recognized her team. For someone who had never practiced mindfulness or knew much about emotional intelligence, Ann's **Reporter** had become adept at labeling her feelings – like disappointment and frustration – and describing the associated unpleasant sensations in her body.

SUZANNE: You're disappointed. What's that experience like?

ANN: My shoulders slump down, my chest caves in, and there's stinging in my chest. I have thoughts like, "He'll never change. I should look for another job." And, behaviorally, I avoid him as much as possible.

SUZANNE: Play a video in your mind of you talking with Nabil when you're disappointed. What are you doing?

ANN: I'm fuming inside, but I'm not telling him that I want him to recognize my team.

SUZANNE: Why would he? That's your job.

ANN: Yeah, but I really want them to get the acknowledgment from higher up than me.

SUZANNE: What's your request of him?

ANN: After we finish this huge software conversion, I want him to give everyone on my team a gift certificate for company inventory. We sell high-end clothing and furniture. Even though our employees get a five percent discount on everything, most of them still can't afford it.

SUZANNE: Is this something that he would normally do?

ANN: No. No way. He's never done that.

SUZANNE: Then, don't expect too much of him. How can you be a Powerful Leader? How can you **Flex Your Style** and be directive with him while also taking on some of the responsibility for the gift certificate?

ANN: Okay, I'll say, "I want you to recognize everyone by giving them a one-time $100 gift certificate for inventory. Here are the numbers on what it could potentially cost the company given their additional five percent discount. However, I think the payback in increased morale will outweigh the cost."

Before their next conversation, Ann did ten minutes of **Mindful Breathing,** then surprised herself when that's exactly what she said to Nabil. No surprise from him; he agreed to do it. Ann made the certificates and arranged a time when all three shifts could attend. Nabil showed up for the short ceremony, recognized everyone, and handed out the certificates. Since not everyone used their certificate, the promotion cost under $2,800, and employees bought beautiful items that made them feel more a part of the company.

SHIFT: Was Nabil a pushover? No, he was a tough cookie – Ann had argued with him for almost a year about various issues. Her story shows how a mindful leader can use the best parts of her boss' style to communicate with him more effectively and get what she wants. At the end of our coaching engagement, I asked Ann what she had gained. "The ability to raise issues. I can directly approach my boss and clear up an issue, so that I don't worry about it or get angry at him." Once she labeled her frustration and disappointment, Ann could take action to be the Calm, Confident, and Powerful Leader she had always wanted to see in a boss.

CONCEPTS

- Listen to and write down your thoughts about your boss. Explore whether those thoughts upset you and limit your behavior and effectiveness.

- Talk with your boss about your style and his style. Pinpoint how your styles are similar and different. Commit to what each of you will do to improve how your styles work together.

- Assess your boss' performance like you would a direct report's performance. Identify to yourself your boss' developmental gaps. How does he need to learn and grow as a professional? In clever ways, encourage him to take risks and practice those new behaviors. Do this by gently pointing out his developmental gaps and by role modeling or teaching those new skills to him.

- Be brave and clever. To move up in an organization, you need to show that you can be direct with your boss and upper management. Even if it's scary to be honest and firm, that's the behavior they want to see. Use the Mindfulness Tools to manage your anxiety or anger. Organizations promote people who have the courage to speak up and hold their ground.

CHAPTER 8

MANAGING DOWN: HOLDING DIRECT REPORTS ACCOUNTABLE

While I want you to recognize how you lead people above and beside you in the organization, most often you're leading people who report directly to you. These three case studies show that a calm, self-assured leader can be successful in even the most challenging conversations with direct reports:

Case Study 1: My co-worker and I competed for a management position; now, I'm her boss.

Case Study 2: A manager who reports to me has no self-confidence.

Case Study 3: One of my faculty members thinks I'm marginalizing him because of his race.

CASE STUDY 1: MY CO-WORKER AND I COMPETED FOR A MANAGEMENT POSITION; NOW, I'M HER BOSS

SITUATION: Rick was a 50-year-old economist, a big guy who played football in high school and college. He was a team leader at a federal agency where his group generated financial trend reports. He and another economist/team lead, Katherine, applied for a management position over the group's four teams. When Rick got the job, Katherine was angry. She was 57, had worked for the agency for 32 years, and had much more technical experience than Rick. It was unusual that each of them wanted to move up in management at a later stage in life. Rick was selected because of his team-leading skills.

One day they were colleagues; the next day, Rick was the boss. Even though Katherine had been around a long time and had designed many of the group's analysis models in the '80s and '90s, her performance had slipped in the last decade. She was resting on her technical reputation rather than continuing to innovate and produce. Unfortunately, none of her previous bosses ever had the courage to call her on it. They let her slack off, read professional journals, and go to conferences.

SYMPTOMS: Rick was excited about leading the division. Due to a shrinking budget, he wanted to prevent layoffs by getting the team leaders to sell analysis services to internal clients at the agency. Unlike her counterparts, Katherine wasn't interested in marketing or creating new projects; she felt that marketing was Rick's job.

As weeks went by and Katherine refused to even try looking for internal clients, Rick became increasingly uncomfortable and reactive to her. He was passively avoiding a direct conversation with Katherine and hoping that peer pressure during the team lead meetings would motivate her to change. That strategy didn't work.

Rick had been Katherine's colleague for many years. Over those years, he was angry with how little she worked and how their bosses let her get by with poor performance. Now that Katherine reported to him, Rick was in a difficult position. He didn't know how to manage his transition from Katherine's colleague to boss, much less know how to hold her accountable for her work.

SOURCE: Rick knew that he lacked confidence and behaved tentatively with Katherine. He allowed her to derail their conversations. Every time Rick brought up her performance, she shifted the topic to technical issues. Because he also let her have the last word, he always walked away with the responsibility for the task or project.

SOLUTION: I told Rick that his mission was to get comfortable with not only his unease but also with Katherine's discomfort. Until Rick could use the Mindfulness Process to **Notice - Breathe - Allow** his physical, mental, emotional, and behavioral distress, he wasn't going to be able to have a successful accountability conversation with Katherine. I also asked him to be clear about his goal and to move from his natural Ask style to telling Katherine how she needed to improve.

Rick developed three goals for his next conversation with Katherine. First, he wanted to explain that the days of unlimited funding had ended and that she needed to find projects and money to keep her team alive. At the same time, he wanted to empathize with Katherine to show that he understood it might initially be challenging for her to learn marketing skills. Second, Rick intended to set a specific deadline for Katherine to find her first new project. Rick's third goal was to *allow* discomfort – his and hers – in the meeting and not let it run his behavior or influence him to take the responsibility from Katherine again.

DON'T FENCE ME IN

Regardless of how she tried to distract him, Rick planned to continually bring the conversation back to Katherine's new job responsibility. When a person looks outside herself for something to distract her from work or even from a conversation, that's a signal to her leader to use the **Tell** approach. I call it "building a fence." Imagine a challenging employee in an open field of grass. If you let the employee go anywhere and do anything she wants, she's going to run wild. She'll define her job duties to fit her needs.

I explained to Rick how to use Katherine's new job description in a very precise Tell approach to build a fence around her. Visualize a small area, about the size of a 12 x 12 foot fenced in area, and use **Laser** statements to calmly corral Katherine back inside the fence. Be mindful. No matter how high you build it, Katherine might jump over the fence and try to run free again. In that case, continue to use the Tell approach to get her back inside.

Rick built the fence using a technique called the "broken record," a Laser statement that you repeat as often as necessary to wake a person up, and let her know, "I am firm on this." Rick's broken record was, "It's up to you." When Katherine resisted with, "I don't know how to do marketing," "There's no place for my team to get another project," or "Maybe you could help me," Rick *noticed* his frustration and fear, then felt his **Feet** on the floor and **Seat** in the chair. When she finished speaking, he calmly hammered a fence post in the ground by replying, "It's up to you." There was no reason for him to feel angry or afraid; he stayed compassionately neutral.

When talking with an employee who was allowed to roam free for many years, a compassionate fence builder has the option to use the Influence Tool of letting her **Vent** a little bit. Because Katherine was used to complaining to her bosses for three decades, she probably wouldn't stop the behavior overnight. Rick told her that he was happy to let her blow off steam for five minutes, then it was up to her to begin marketing her team.

Regarding venting, I recommended a maximum five minute time frame to Rick. If you like, make it a little fun by setting a timer. Also, request that each complaint be new material. Without that rule, you'll hear repetitive whining. If she slips up and repeats a complaint, gently interrupt to remind her that you already captured that concern. Setting these boundaries will keep your conversations shorter and more solution-focused.

SHIFT: Before our next call, I got a good news email from Rick. "After just two conversations, Katherine has shown huge improvements in her behavior and is nearly fully funded for the next fiscal year." It might sound hard to believe, but when you build a fence for folks, most of them appreciate it. Many resistant employees are exhausted from being able to roam around wherever they wanted to. They actually want you to set limits for them, because boundaries help them be successful.

Rick's super success story demonstrates a five-step process for holding someone accountable. You'll see the Influence Process steps – **Speak - Observe - Focus** – in brackets:

1. Set a clear goal in your mind. [**Speak - Observe - Focus** your goal to yourself]

2. Clearly communicate that goal to the other person's mind. [*Speak* to other person]

3. Check that she understands and is ready to take action on the goal by asking **Open-Ended Questions**: [*Observe* other person's reaction]

   a. "What is your understanding of what I expect you to do?"

   b. "What's the first step you will take?"

   c. "How and when will you do that?"

   d. "What barriers do you expect, and how will you overcome them?"

4. Communicate verbally and nonverbally that you will hold her accountable for the goal. When she tries to distract the conversation, stay calm, and use a broken record to bring her mind back to the goal. [*Focus* other person on your goal]

5. Schedule a series of brief follow-up meetings within one to three days of each other to check for and acknowledge progress. Over time, the meetings will become shorter and less frequent as she takes on the responsibility for holding herself accountable. [*Focus* other person on your goal].

Rick said that thorough planning was the key to his success. Before the conversation, he wrote down his goals, follow-up questions, and broken record so that he knew exactly what he would say regardless of Katherine's resistance. He took his notes into the meeting and calmly referred to them during the conversation, using **Feet & Seat** whenever he felt nervous. Katherine responded positively.

I asked Rick to assess our first few coaching conversations. "Coaching got me to crystallize my goals for resolving a problem and write down how to reach those goals. I helped change the behavior of a direct report in a rapid way by having meetings with her specifically focused on changing one negative behavior."

It's important to *focus* on one behavior at a time. Don't go into a meeting with a laundry list of issues that you want fixed. When Rick *focused* on Katherine's marketing behavior, he helped her turn it around immediately.

He also said about coaching, "It forces a manager to become introspective, to understand the link between emotions and management style." This is an impressive insight for a leader who hadn't previously practiced mindfulness or thought about his or his direct reports' emotions. Once Rick applied **Notice - Breathe - Allow** to his own anxiety and reluctance to hold Katherine accountable, he saw his emotions as a helpful warning signal. "Now, I list everything I consider a management issue on a daily basis and examine my emotions about each item before taking action."

Rick also developed a consistent mindfulness practice. He began doing 20 to 30 minutes of silent practice every night in his backyard. Within a matter of weeks, Rick was sleeping better, and his blood pressure had dropped. Taking time for intrapersonal attunement enhanced his health and helped Rick become more aware of his Calm, Confident, and Powerful leadership behaviors.

CASE STUDY NUMBER 2: A MANAGER WHO REPORTS TO ME HAS NO SELF-CONFIDENCE

SITUATION: At 41, Charlie was a former Army lieutenant colonel with very high expectations of himself and others. On the executive fast track at an alternative energy firm, Charlie was recently promoted to director of information technology with three managers reporting to him. He quickly diagnosed that one of his managers, Jim, had some serious performance problems.

SYMPTOMS: When Charlie set an expectation, Jim didn't report back to him on the status in a timely manner. The bigger problem: Jim was a "yes" man. Charlie was a self-assured leader and not threatened by people who disagreed with him. He wanted his managers to be independent thinkers, so he was irritated when Jim never questioned him or questioned his assignments in order to protect Jim's staff. Charlie suspected that Jim was afraid to speak his mind, because he feared some kind of job reprisal. However, Charlie wasn't that kind of leader.

Charlie described his failed attempts with Jim.

> CHARLIE: I've tried being direct and saying, "Look, I want you to disagree with me." I've tried talking with all three of my managers

as a group and asking them to question me and disagree with me. The other managers do it, but Jim still nods "yes" to everything I say.

SUZANNE: What do you tell yourself are the underlying causes of Jim's behavior?

CHARLIE: Jim just hasn't had enough success in the past, and he lacks self-confidence. How can I teach Jim to be more assured?

It's an interesting question. Unfortunately, you can't tell someone, "Hey, your ideas are good," and expect it to stick in his mind. People need to experience confidence from the inside as a result of intrapersonal attunement. The challenge is how to help someone have an inner experience of self-confidence so that he tells himself and everyone else, "My ideas are great!"

SOURCE: On our next call, Charlie said that he started the most recent management team meeting by explaining, "When I finish talking about this topic, I'm going to ask each of you to tell me one thing I said that you question or disagree with." The other two managers were responsive and felt comfortable disagreeing with Charlie. When it was Jim's turn, he agreed with everything that Charlie had said. Though Charlie was irritated, he passively let Jim get by without disagreeing.

It's common for a leader to focus so much external energy on trying to fix other people that it prevents him from seeing internally how he is part of the problem. During our conversation, Charlie acknowledged how his own behavioral pattern of allowing Jim to agree with him all the time was stalling Jim's growth. It was time for some tough love. Well, not love, leadership.

SOLUTION: Charlie and I discussed how to get more information from Jim about what he thought was an appropriate level of disagreement with a superior. I suggested that they talk about Jim's perceptions of what it meant to disagree or be in conflict with Charlie. Charlie emailed me a few days later to say that the conversation didn't work either. He still wasn't seeing the confidence in Jim's behavior that he wanted to.

At this point, the corporation began going through a major audit. Most of Charlie's department was stressed about the increasing workloads and deadlines. Charlie started noticing unusual behavior in several people and particularly in Jim. One of Jim's direct reports was under investigation for inappropriate behavior. Even though the legal implications for her and the department were severe, Jim wasn't keeping information about the case confidential. He talked about it with people on his team despite being part of the formal grievance process.

Charlie knew that he had to take swift action. He put Jim on probation and used the **BEER** formula to deliver a strong message: "I acknowledge the pressure that the audit and grievance are causing for everyone. But, when you convey information that should be held in strict confidence [Behavior], I have trouble trusting your behavior right now [Effect], and I feel angry and nervous [Emotions]. Those conversations must stop [Requirement]."

STINKIN' THINKIN'

At this point, Charlie assumed that Jim wouldn't make it through the probationary period and would have to be replaced. In our next call, Charlie wanted to use Exploration to discuss his negative thought, "Jim has low self-confidence." He *noticed* that when he had that thought, he overreacted and treated Jim as though he was incompetent. For example, Charlie over-explained assignments and asked patronizing questions like, "Are you sure you understand what I'm saying?"

Charlie's mind was like a lawyer who could only see evidence that supported his case. It was so busy collecting evidence of Jim's low confidence that it couldn't see examples of when Jim acted decisively. After doing The Work©, Charlie's **Reporter** learned to quickly *notice* when he was having negative thoughts about Jim. As a result, his mind stopped looking for proof of low confidence and began seeing the ways in which Jim displayed self-assurance.

For example, one day, Jim disagreed with Charlie and said, "I'm not convinced of your idea." There were also cases of Jim being direct with an employee by stating a clear expectation. Those examples helped Charlie's mind begin to widen its lens and *affirm*, "Sometimes, Jim does have self confidence." As a result, Charlie started acknowledging Jim, "I liked it when you set the deadline for Mary." Charlie's affirmations could help Jim *notice* his own success and continue to change his behavior.

"EARTH TO JIM, EARTH TO JIM"

This was important, because I was sensing that Jim was unaware of his behavior. His **Reporter** was on a permanent vacation and not sending any news updates from himself to himself about himself. I suggested that as part of the performance expectation plan, Charlie require that Jim keep an **Awareness Log** to help him develop mindfulness on the job.

In our next coaching session, Charlie reported, "I worked with Jim on methods to monitor his behavior. He developed a log for tracking each time he either stopped himself from making a near miss or caught himself demonstrating an effective behavior. I also set an expectation that he manage his direct reports more closely and give me a daily update." Charlie role-modeled the Powerful Leader behaviors that he wanted to see in Jim: setting firm expectations and holding people accountable.

"THIS IS GROUND CONTROL TO MAJOR JIM"

Perhaps being put on probation made Jim sit up and take notice. He not only wanted to keep his job, he wanted to succeed and be considered for advancement at some point down the road. After Charlie made it very clear what was expected of him, Jim began working one on one with his team members to address their performance issues – similar to how Charlie had worked with him. Jim kept a log of his interactions with direct reports, colleagues, and Charlie. Simply writing down his behaviors and the impact they had on others turned Jim's performance around in a matter of weeks. He even got comfortable disagreeing with Charlie on a regular basis.

I asked Charlie to reward Jim's quick turnaround and to encourage Jim to begin rewarding himself. It was great that Charlie could direct, encourage, monitor, and reward him. Next, it was time for Jim to begin doing those behaviors for himself.

SHIFT: Charlie was surprised by Jim's quick turnaround. When I asked what he learned from the experience, Charlie talked about the Mindfulness Process of **Notice - Breathe - Allow**. "I understand the deeper nature of stress and worry, and how my thoughts impact my behavior. Now, when I get frustrated with my managers, I see two things – the part I play in the situation and that I'm only *noticing* how they disappoint me. That helps me open the lens wider to see what they're also doing well and how I can change my approach."

When I asked Charlie how he was behaving differently with his employees, he said, "I was pretty forthright in communication anyway, but since our coaching, I am even more direct, especially when someone is not meeting my expectations. My fear of how people might respond negatively to me was much worse than how they do react."

CASE STUDY 3: ONE OF MY FACULTY MEMBERS THINKS I'M MARGINALIZING HIM BECAUSE OF HIS RACE

SITUATION: Britt was the 62-year-old chair of the art department in a small liberal arts college in Massachusetts. She had 12 full-time and 5 part-time faculty members in her department. When she arrived in her new position from a university in Florida, she heard a lot of gossip about Harlen, a 56-year-old faculty member in the department. According to the grapevine:

• His approaches to art and teaching were outdated.

• As a member of the Navajo Nation, he felt victimized no matter how well he was treated.

• He talked in a circular style that few people understood.

In order to be open-minded and connect with Harlen, Britt decided that she needed to learn about his culture. During her first year on the job, she read books about Navajo culture, listened to Native American radio, and talked candidly with a Native American professor from a neighboring college. After a year of "study," she felt confident and even a little proud that she had gained a great deal of sensitivity to Harlen's style of communicating and teaching.

SYMPTOMS: At the end of the year, Britt was stunned and insulted when she received an angry, three-page, single-spaced letter from Harlen accusing her of marginalizing him. There were several biting remarks in the letter, including suggesting that Britt should try helping all, rather than some, of the department faculty. She was shocked and deeply hurt.

Harlen was irate that Britt hadn't invited him to be on a search committee for the department's new faculty position. She hadn't even asked his opinion about the candidates.

Britt was livid. Not only had Harlen never indicated his interest in being on the committee, she'd sent emails to all faculty encouraging their feedback on the candidates.

SOURCE: After listening to her vent about the letter for a while, I asked how this situation reflected a pattern in her work or personal life. Britt replied, "I've spent most of my life, in both personal and professional relationships, trying to figure out how to do exactly the right and honorable thing in every situation for each person—which is admirable but unrealistic – especially when I don't know, let alone understand, the other person's perspective!"

SOLUTION: Britt had a very strong mindfulness practice, and she was skilled at talking about even the most challenging leadership experiences. Over the previous four months, we had already done coaching on other leadership issues and had developed a trusting relationship. I knew it was appropriate to give her strong feedback about the letter.

SUZANNE: What Harlen's saying is true.

BRITT: Really?! I hope you're kidding.

SUZANNE: It's true for him.

BRITT (Long pause as she used **Notice - Breathe - Allow** to experience her response to my comment): It is true for him, of course. I disagree with Harlen, but that's not really the point, is it? It's true for him that I was marginalizing him, and he's telling me that he's angry and hurt about that.

A PLAN

Britt developed a three-part plan for her conversation with Harlen. For part one, Britt read each issue carefully and calmly on Harlen's list of complaints. Then, she wrote down what she felt he was trying to express using **Facts & Feelings** statements. For example, she wrote, "You're angry, because I didn't invite you to be a member of the search committee," and, "You feel marginalized, because I didn't ask you for feedback on the candidates." Even though the last statement wasn't true in Britt's mind, she understood that it was true in his mind.

In Britt's second step, she considered how to respond to the "facts" of each issue. She decided that during their conversation, she wouldn't initially defend herself or correct Harlen on the "facts." If she felt a complaint was true, she would agree with him.

If a complaint wasn't true in her mind, she would wait until later in the conversation to ask **Open-Ended Questions** and find out what happened to make him feel it was true. Britt didn't want to reactively disagree by saying, "You're wrong about that." Instead, she planned to first explain and then ask, "I had a different experience and a different intention than how you see it. May I tell you how I saw it?" Asking permission gives the other person the chance to prepare his mind for new information that will conflict with his beliefs.

"May I tell you about it?" might sound like a patronizing or rhetorical question. However, when asked with a sincere, calm voice, it shows respect to the other person. Don't ask it, unless you're willing to accept the answers, "No" or "No, I'd like to wait for another time to hear about that." If you get either response, reply with, "That's fine. I was open to hearing your side of the situation. When, within the next few days, will you be ready to hear my side?" Don't let the disagreement drag on. If the other person continues to delay hearing your side of the story, be firm, and set a time for follow-up with, "I want to have our next discussion tomorrow at 2:00."

For the third part of Britt's plan, she would ask Harlen if he could suggest a few things she could do differently that would help him feel more included and respected. She also planned to thank Harlen for sending the letter, because it gave her the opportunity for professional growth. Britt practiced her side of the conversation in her head several times. Then, she asked Harlen if she could come to his office to talk about his letter. She set a time at the end of the day when they could talk as long as necessary.

A MEETING OF THE MINDS

In our next call, Britt said she started the conversation by saying, "Harlen, I'm glad that you wrote the letter. At first, I was very upset, but I read it several times and really thought about it. I want to make sure that I understood you by telling you what I heard you say in the letter. Please correct anything I say if it isn't absolutely what you intended to communicate."

Britt said that as she summarized each of his points, Harlen started to smile. She was surprised, because she expected him to stay angry. He said, "Yes, that's exactly right" as she continued. Then, they discussed each issue on his list. By the end of the 2 ½ hour conversation, they had two agreements: (1) when she wanted his active participation in a task or project, Britt would invite him, in person, rather than by email, and (2) when he wanted to be a part of a project, Harlen would let her know directly.

SHIFT: After the conversation, Britt emailed me this summary: "My experience with Harlen and with coaching helped me realize that when someone is angry with me, it's much more valuable to listen, apologize, and make changes rather than get angry and defensive. I realized that I can handle a very difficult situation with grace. I now see that there's a huge payoff to being open to the 'truth' of what anyone says to me and to responding with compassion. I feel much less afraid of disapproval and conflict. As a result, I think my 'vibe' as a leader is much more confident, relaxed, and present."

CONCEPTS

- Thorough planning is the key to success in a difficult conversation. Before the conversation, write down your specific goal as a **Laser Message** as well as any support statements or **Open-Ended Questions**. Commit to achieving your goal regardless of the physical, mental, emotional, or behavioral discomfort that you or the other person experience during the meeting.

- When a direct report tries to divert a conversation, build a mental fence to *focus* her mind on your expectation. Calmly repeat a broken record – your bottom line – as often as necessary to let her know that you aren't giving in. For example, "It's up to you," "That's no longer an option," "What's your solution?" or "This is your responsibility."

- Fine-tune your **Reporter** so that it picks up on your negative judgments about your direct reports. Use Exploration to *listen* to your complaints as quickly as possible. Write them down, and investigate them. Notice how your mind actively seeks proof of your judgment to the exclusion of what the person is also doing well. When you're finished investigating your thoughts, *affirm* what is true and make an action plan to influence the situation in a positive way.

- Rather than get upset when someone judges you, become curious and ask about the reasoning behind her opinion. Explain your side of the story. Make specific agreements on how each of you will change your behavior to improve your working relationship.

CHAPTER 9

MANAGING ACROSS:
FACILITATING EFFECTIVE AGREEMENTS

Even though you don't have formal power over your co-workers and colleagues, you can still use The Mind to Lead model to influence them. These case studies show how three of my coaching clients were assertive – without being aggressive or insensitive – with colleagues. Each case shows how they used one of The Mind to Lead processes – Mindfulness, Exploration, or Influence – to be more effective.

Case Study 1 on Staying Calm: I can't say no to a professional peer.

Case Study 2 on Being Confident: My colleagues are wimps.

Case Study 3 on Using Power: My team is ignoring me.

CASE STUDY 1 ON STAYING CALM: I CAN'T SAY NO TO A PROFESSIONAL PEER

This case shows how to stay calm using the Mindfulness Steps: **Notice - Breathe - Allow.**

SITUATION: Michael was the 45-year-old chief of a large bureau in a federal agency. He was a recognized leader in his field and volunteered on many committees that required a large amount of time. As part of his job, he frequently did public speaking and was very inspirational. His talks always led to more requests for appearances and projects, all of which was uncompensated as a federal employee.

Michael had trouble saying "No" to requests from colleagues and consumers that he either didn't have time for or wasn't interested in doing. He passively consented, because he was afraid to disappoint people or make them mad at his bureau. When he reluctantly said, "Yes," he was angry at himself for agreeing.

SYMPTOMS: When we began our coaching engagement, I asked him to write a measurable goal statement of what he wanted to achieve. He wrote, "To better say 'No' to people without paying a price for it professionally or personally."

When he was younger, Michael was able to do a lot of professional volunteer work. He enjoyed being involved in a variety of initiatives in his field. He believed his time on the projects was important and would lead to his professional success.

The situation had changed. Michael felt that he could no longer help on projects that didn't directly benefit his bureau. While his boss expected him to keep a positive public image and contribute to the field, he was concerned that Michael was experiencing burnout and losing his temper more with his staff.

When I asked how he would know he was successful in achieving his goal, Michael replied, "By how much I can limit things that I shouldn't be doing, by how well I can maintain the relationship with a person I say 'No' to, and by how much fun I have learning this new process."

SOURCE: When someone made a request of him before, Michael would say something indirect such as, "Wow, that would be great to do, but I need to take a rain check on that." When I asked how that response sounded to him now, Michael said, "It's ambiguous. When I take a rain check, it means the person can come back later. And, that's what people do. They ask me again later to do the project. Eventually, I give in, but I'm mad that I agree to do it."

SOLUTION: I asked Michael for a good organizing principle to help him decide whether to say, "Yes" or "No" to a request.

> MICHAEL: My decision should be driven by my organization's strategic plan. My boss says if it's on paper, I have to get it done.

> SUZANNE: What's a Laser statement that shows your appreciation to the requester while also setting a boundary?

> MICHAEL: That's an exciting project that doesn't fit with what I need to accomplish in my strategic plan.

As he began using the **Laser** statement, people appreciated his honesty and directness. Sometimes, he offered the name of someone else who could help or he asked an **Open-Ended Question** to help find an alternative solution: "How could you use your current resources to accomplish that without me?" Michael noticed that Lasering protected him and his staff, while also allowing him to role model healthy boundaries.

LET ME DOWN EASY

On our next call, Michael was nervous about an upcoming meeting with a colleague, Gina. Several months earlier, Gina asked him to serve on a national policy committee that would make their field more visible. Michael mentioned the initiative to his boss who expected him to get involved. Michael was conflicted. While the agenda was interesting, he didn't have time, yet, he said yes. Now he was worried, because he was attending a professional association meeting in Chicago the following week with Gina and several other colleagues who wanted him on the committee.

As we talked, Michael outlined the steps he would take to remove himself from the commitment. First, he would tell his boss that he was turning down the invitation to focus on the strategic plan. Next, he wrote his goals for the conversation with Gina:

- Express his appreciation that Gina and others wanted him involved.
- Remove himself from the committee.
- Explain that he hoped this wouldn't negatively impact either their professional relationship or their personal friendship.

MINDFULNESS STEPS STEP 1: NOTICE

As Michael planned for the conversation, I asked him to reflect on past interactions with Gina and the communication patterns they developed. Michael said, "When Gina asks me to do something, I listen and try to figure out a way to be able to meet her request. Then, when I accommodate her, she advances further and asks for more. When she advances, I say something sarcastic like, 'Whoa, when's it going to stop? You could squeeze blood out of a turnip.' I'm mad at that point, but I don't know how to express it."

To help him stay calm and not give in to Gina, I suggested that he spend five minutes doing a mindfulness practice before the meeting. He liked the idea, and said he could arrive at the conference room early to practice **Feet & Seat** before the others arrived. Staying calm and maintaining some intrapersonal attunement during the conversation would help him *notice* the physical, mental, and emotional discomfort that drove him to say, "Yes."

MINDFULNESS STEPS STEP 2: BREATHE

Next, we talked about how Michael could set a firm boundary early in the conversation.

SUZANNE: How could you completely change your communication pattern with Gina?

MICHAEL: I could proactively bring up the issue rather than wait until she mentions it. Once Gina starts talking, she advances so quickly that it overwhelms me. I don't know how to stop her or say, "No."

SUZANNE: When do you need to remember to take a breath with a long exhalation?

MICHAEL: Right before I bring up the topic and just before I deliver my **Laser Message**.

SUZANNE: What's your **Laser Message**?

MICHAEL: A variation on my basic theme. It'll be, "Thank you for inviting me; unfortunately it doesn't fit with my organization's strategic priorities."

SUZANNE: Sounds good. I suggest that as soon as you finish your Laser statement, you return to the mindful breaths with long exhalations. Those will remind you to **Pause** and wait for Gina's response instead of jumping in to save her.

MICHAEL: Will do.

MINDFULNESS STEPS STEP 3: ALLOW

SUZANNE: What are some possible responses she might have?

MICHAEL: I've never tried to resist her much, but when I do, she usually goes silent. I'm so uncomfortable with dead air that I fill up the space by caving in and agreeing to whatever she wants.

SUZANNE: What do you need to *allow* so that you can remain

silent while she thinks it over?

MICHAEL: I need to *notice* and *allow* my discomfort in the four realms. In particular, I need to *allow* my scary thoughts, which might sound something, like, "She's getting mad at me. I'm letting the profession down. She needs my help. I should say 'Yes.'"

SUZANNE: Where do you tend to feel those kinds of thoughts in your body?

MICHAEL: My stomach and chest. Both get really tense.

SUZANNE: Play a video in your mind right now of Gina being silent and you having those thoughts. Can you feel those tense sensations now?

MICHAEL: Yes, it's not as strong, but I can sense the pressure.

SUZANNE: Good. Sit with those sensations for a minute. *Allow* them to be in your body, and *notice* what happens as you scan your awareness through the tension.

MICHAEL: The sensations are still there, but they've lessened to about a quarter of their original strength. This is a helpful rehearsal to see that I won't die from the tension. I'll just wait her out. And, whatever she says, I'll remember to take a few moments to **Notice - Breathe - Allow** before I speak.

SUZANNE: It sounds like you're ready, Michael.

When I asked Michael on our next call how it went with Gina, he said, "I feel liberated. It was very easy to follow my plan, because it was so specific. I brought up the topic at the end of the meeting, because I wanted my other colleagues to hear the conversation, too. When I delivered my **Laser Message**, Gina went silent. I got pretty uncomfortable! Luckily, I was able to *notice*, *breathe*, and *allow* the discomfort. I looked around the table, and my peers were mute. Finally, Gina said that she understood and accepted my decision. She didn't press me or say anything pushy. It felt great!"

SHIFT: On our last call, Michael reported he had become more realistic about what he could take on. He also was much more aware of the words he spoke and what he promised to others.

SUZANNE: Those are excellent accomplishments on the outside. How has your experience changed on the inside?

MICHAEL: I feel fantastic. I have much more energy, because now my mind is so focused on my strategic plan and the bureau's success. My mind doesn't feel frenetic like when I was taking on everything and afraid to say, "No." People respect that I'm setting boundaries with them. Instead of being mad at me, they're even more drawn to our organization's work.

SUZANNE: That's outstanding. What has your boss noticed?

MICHAEL: He commented recently that I'm coming across with a much more realistic, systematic, and less emotional leadership style. I get why you call it Calm, Confident Power.

SUZANNE: Any word from Gina?

MICHAEL: No more requests. Though I did have a pleasant email exchange with her recently about baseball season. She's a Yankees fan, and I'm a Braves fan. I'm amazed that it only took one, relatively easy conversation to set a firm boundary with her. I think she got the message on a broader level that she can't turn to me every time she needs help.

CASE STUDY 2 ON BEING CONFIDENT: MY COLLEAGUES ARE WIMPS

This case shows how to be confident using the Exploration Steps: **Listen - Inquire - Affirm.**

SITUATION: Letisha was one of six division heads who reported to the deputy mayor for Economic Development of a major U.S. city. Three managers reported to her. A month after she was promoted to division head of Small Business Services, word came down that the budget for one of her programs would be reduced 15 percent.

The executive team who reported to the deputy mayor – on which Letisha now served – proposed that Max, a web designer on the team, would have to be let go. While Letisha was upset about losing Max, she agreed with the plan. She wanted to give Max as much advance notice as possible, hoping that he could find a position somewhere else in city government.

SYMPTOMS: Unfortunately, the rest of the executive team felt that the deputy mayor, Andrew, should personally lay off Max. Over the next four months, the executive team had tedious discussions on how to implement the layoff without alarming the other employees. That's right, four months and no announcement. Letisha was astounded at how much time they were wasting in the bi-weekly meetings. Moreover, she was incredibly frustrated by the delay in action. She was upset about having to lay Max off. However, she knew it should be done quickly as a professional courtesy to him and as a way to stay on budget once the new fiscal year started. She'd worked at the city for eight years and had been enthusiastic about building her career there. Nevertheless, the stalled layoff was disappointing and disillusioning.

SOURCE: It was at this point that Letisha hired me as her coach. When she explained the situation, I recognized her lack of confidence to speak up. We talked about how this pattern had surfaced before in her work. There were several critical points in her career when she didn't speak up in fear of rocking the boat. I explained the Exploration Steps to Letisha as a way to cultivate confidence as a leader: **Listen - Inquire - Affirm**.

EXPLORATION STEPS STEP 1: LISTEN

First, I asked Letisha to *listen* to the reasons that she told herself the process had stalled. Her **Reporter** did a great job identifying thoughts that were all over the map:

- "It's not my job to push this process; my boss should be in charge."
- "My boss is uncomfortable firing Max."
- "I haven't been a division head long enough to speak up."
- "The rest of the executive team is more experienced than me; I should defer to their decision."
- "These people are incompetent."

I also asked her to *listen* to her strong feelings. She felt powerless spending hours in unproductive meetings where she sensed everyone was in denial about what needed to happen. And, she was angry that delaying the inevitable was costing the city in lost efficiency and employee stress. Everyone deserved to know what was going to happen, and the rumor mill was cranking out some scary misinformation.

EXPLORATION STEPS STEP 2: INQUIRE

Once Letisha could hear her thoughts and feelings, she could question what was true and investigate how her inner experience impacted her behavior.

SOLUTION: I asked Letisha if she had ever pointed out in a meeting that the group wasn't making progress. Her reply: "It's not my place to speak up. Besides, they wouldn't listen to me."

Through a series of questions adapted from The Work© by Byron Katie, I helped Letisha *inquire* about whether those negative beliefs were true.

> SUZANNE: Is it, in fact, inappropriate for you to speak up?
>
> LETISHA: Maybe not. I see what needs to happen more clearly than anyone else on the team.
>
> SUZANNE: Are you 100 percent sure that no one will listen to you?
>
> LETISHA: No, I don't have a crystal ball that can tell me exactly what people will do.
>
> SUZANNE: How does the belief, "They won't listen to me," impact your feelings and behavior?
>
> LETISHA: When I have that thought in meetings, I feel a mixture of afraid, sad, and angry. The combination of those thoughts and feelings makes me sit motionless and mute.

EXPLORATION STEPS STEP 3: AFFIRM

Doing The Work© on her negative thoughts allowed Letisha to see that she was imagining a scary future. Those thoughts were destroying her confidence and immobilizing her. After she questioned what was true, Letisha could calmly *affirm* what she wanted. She was clear that it was her responsibility to take action.

I asked Letisha to develop a broken record for the next executive meeting that she would repeat as often as needed to take her teammates out of their passivity trance. She developed, "We need a date to lay off Max." At the end of our coaching session, she didn't believe she would have the guts to actually say it, however, I invited her to be the change agent that she wanted her boss and colleagues to be. I encouraged her to use **Mindful Breathing** or **Feet & Seat** to stay calm when she spoke up.

On our next call, Letisha reported that the next executive meeting got off track as usual. A few individuals talked too much, and the group made no progress on the layoff plan. Letisha *listened* to her thoughts and feelings during the meeting. When she noticed right away that she was upset, she decided it was worth the risk to try her broken record at least once or twice. In a calm, firm voice, she said, "We need a date to lay off Max."

You can imagine the heads turning and eyes squinting at Letisha. What happened next? Everyone agreed with her. One calm sentence snapped them out of the trance and gave her immediate influence in the group. Letisha was stunned and delighted that it worked the first time. "We got a lot further than I imagined. We set a date and made a plan for me to lay off Max."

Lucky for Letisha and her team that she stepped up. Within two weeks of her displaying Calm, Confident Power, the city got more bad news about reduced tax revenue projections. Thanks to Letisha, the executive team was already in motion. Within a week, they rolled out a major reorganization including three more layoffs. The executive team asked Letisha to handle all of the layoff conversations. Her confidence was so high that she agreed to do it.

In our coaching session before the layoff conversations, I asked Letisha to *listen* (Step 1) to her fears and concerns about delivering the bad news to employees:

- "They're going to argue and ask, 'Why me?'"
- "They're going to blame me."
- "They won't be able to find new jobs."

Using Step 2, Letisha *inquired* about what was true. She was nervous but also excited about helping each individual cope with the job loss in an open, calm way. She planned what she would say and how she would handle any pushback from the employees. In case anyone was particularly resistant, she wrote a broken record to *affirm* (Step 3) what she wanted: "It's understandable you're upset, however let's focus on helping you move forward." In our next coaching session, Letisha reported that none of the four people fought back. Letisha's biggest surprise in the whole process was that the people who got the most upset were the ones who kept their jobs; their guilt made it difficult to watch others leave the city.

SHIFT: Downsizing has a reputation for being traumatic on everyone. However, Letisha noticed that most of her stress came from imagining a horrible future rather than experiencing anything bad. Fear fantasies paralyze leaders. The Exploration Steps let her see that her fearful thoughts weren't true. Our final coaching session celebrated her success.

SUZANNE: What did you learn?

LETISHA: I learned so much. I assumed the worse, but it didn't happen. Just because my boss and colleagues had managed layoffs before, they weren't any more confident than I am. I have to go with my gut and step up when the situation calls for it. And, as far as the employees are concerned, I should give people more credit for how they handle difficult changes.

SUZANNE: What was your biggest take away from coaching?

LETISHA: I can solve problems. When I identify problems that I want someone else to fix, I now realize that I can do it myself.

SUZANNE: How have you changed as a leader?

LETISHA: I've increased my confidence significantly regarding my interactions in meetings. I'm not always right, but that's okay because of my overall positive impact and contribution. My self-esteem is back, and I'm able to make decisions that are right on.

CASE STUDY 3 ON SHOWING POWER: MY TEAM IS IGNORING ME

This case shows how to use power appropriately with the Influence Steps: **Speak - Observe - Focus**.

SITUATION: Bill was 58 years old and worked as a contractor at one of the major

U.S.-based international aid organizations. National headquarters put him on special database projects that none of the staff knew how to do. The organization was concerned about his communication style, which many people experienced as angry. They had considered ending his contract because of his temper, yet didn't want to lose their investment in his knowledge base.

Even though he wasn't an employee, the company paid for his coaching in hopes that Bill would change his aggressive behavior. I rarely take on clients like Bill for two reasons. First, coaching works best when the individual – not the organization – decides to engage in the process. Second, Bill's behavior wasn't an issue of getting upset once in awhile; he was angry and intimidating a lot of the time. My work is most successful with anxious, not angry, leaders.

I made it clear in our first meeting that coaching has a limited reach and doesn't address psychological issues. I asked Bill to hire a therapist, concurrent with our coaching, to help him address the source of his anger.

Bill's goal for our coaching engagement was, "To change my communication style so that it fosters cooperation and self worth rather than resentment in the people I communicate with." I was impressed that the goal wasn't just about how he was going to experience less stress. He wanted other people to have a more positive experience of him.

SYMPTOMS: Bill summed up the pain he was experiencing in one sentence: "I'm my own worst enemy; I'm a perfectionist."

SOURCE: Unfortunately, when a person has unusually high expectations of himself, he tends to project those expectations on other people. Not only did Bill want to be perfect, he expected other people to be flawless, too.

SOLUTION: Internally, The Work© helped Bill a great deal with his negative thoughts and emotions about people. The second step was giving him a communication tool that would let him express his strong emotions and make requests of people in a non-confrontational way so that he could get his needs met.

INFLUENCE STEPS STEP 1: SPEAK

Bill was invited to be on a team that was developing new information processing benchmarks. He attended the first meeting, though he missed three subsequent meetings, because his client boss, Ross, scheduled the meetings when Bill wasn't available.

Bill liked the **BEER** formula. He decided to use it to express his concern about being pushed out of meetings on the new project. He wrote these statements before the next meeting:

- **BEHAVIOR**: "The last three benchmark meetings were scheduled when I'm working with another team in your organization."
- **EFFECT**: "I need to know the issues on this project, so that I can develop an effective database."
- **EMOTION**: "I feel frustrated and disappointed when meetings are scheduled when I'm with another group."
- **REQUEST**: "I request that my calendar be taken into account whenever possible for future meetings on this project."

Fortunately, he was able to attend the next meeting. Though he was nervous about bringing it up, Bill took a deep breath and began to *speak* his **BEER** statements to the team.

INFLUENCE STEPS STEP 2: OBSERVE

About half way into his message, Ross, his client boss, cut Bill off and began defending the decision to schedule the meetings without Bill. Bill did a quick intrapersonal and interpersonal attunement check. He *observed* tension in his chest and angry thoughts in his mind. He also *noticed* that Ross and the others were moving the conversation past Bill's request. So, he decided to drop the topic and feel his breath so that he could relax.

INFLUENCE STEPS STEP 3: FOCUS

As the meeting was coming to an end, Bill *observed* the mood in the room lightening up. He decided that it was a good time to focus his colleagues' minds on his issue again. He calmly stated, "I'd like permission to complete my request without it being heard as a complaint." Ross apologized for cutting Bill off earlier in the meeting, and said that he would be willing to listen to his request. Bill delivered his full BEER statement in a calm voice. When Bill finished, Ross explained that he told people to schedule the meetings without Bill, because Ross planned to relay the information to Bill. While Bill wasn't happy to hear that, at least he got an explanation for being left out.

Bill summarized the outcome of the meeting, "I requested that Ross please consider my calendar for these meetings. As a result, the weekly meetings were rescheduled, so that I was able to attend. I emphasized that I wasn't making a demand, rather a request that was important to me. It'll probably take some time to turn the use of BEER into a habit, though I certainly can't argue with the results."

SHIFT: In our last coaching conversation, Bill talked about the specific tools he learned to relax his inner experience and then communicate his requests to people. He noticed that using the BEER formula as well as The Work© reduced much of his physical, mental, and emotional stress so that he could be more effective in his work.

Bill said it hurt that Ross was trying to edge him out of meetings, because he felt Bill's communication style was impeding team effectiveness. However, Bill's calm commitment to improving his behavior eventually got Ross' attention and acceptance. Bill learned to be honest and direct, and the BEER formula helped him be a more effective team member.

CONCEPTS

- Write a strategic plan or annual goals to clarify your priorities. Use that document to establish clear boundaries in your mind and on your to-do list about tasks and projects that you can and can't take on. Say, "No, thank you" to requests that don't further those goals.

- When you're in a meeting, *notice* your body sensations, thoughts, and feelings and their impact on your behavior or lack of it. Identify how you want to change your behavior to help you get your needs met. When you feel frustrated, say one neutral sentence in the meeting that describes what is currently happening and how you want it to change.

- Use the **BEER** formula in meetings to make a request. If people don't respond or they shut you out, use mindfulness to regain a sense of calm. Ask permission later in that meeting or in a subsequent meeting to complete your request without being interrupted.

CONCLUSION

LEAD YOUR MIND

If you read this book, it's because you care as much about how you get results as the results you get. You know that it's not only possible to achieve organizational goals while being non-confrontational and fair; you know that it's necessary. And, you understand that leading is as much about guiding and motivating yourself as it is about impacting others. As a result, you continuously learn and grow. You enjoy being self-reflective and are open to constructive feedback. You also seek out new information and ideas, for example the emerging field of neuroleadership and how scientific findings about the brain can help leaders be more effective.

The foundation of being more effective is simply noticing. Being willing and having the skills to see yourself and others as we really are can lessen the natural reactivity of the mind. Mindfulness is the tool that helps you notice. When you engage the prefrontal cortex in mindfulness, the mind lets go of the scary narrative, comes back to experiencing what's happening right now, and relaxes a bit.

To develop this Calm Leader mindset, you can use the Mindfulness process to *notice*, *breathe*, and *allow* whatever is happening in your body, thoughts, feelings, and actions. Perhaps you recall Michael's story of managing across and his reluctance to say "no" to Gina's requests for help. Those few moments of intrapersonal attunement – checking in with himself to notice his tendency to want to say "yes," taking a breath, and allowing his discomfort – relaxed his mind and reminded him to pause rather than jump in to save her.

Similarly, when Karen was talking with Randall about his inappropriate comment in the team meeting, she used intrapersonal attunement to stay calm despite his reactivity. Then, she added the process of interpersonal attunement to reflect back her best guess about what was happening for him. As Randall felt seen and heard and realized that he wasn't in trouble with Karen, he eventually calmed down and could talk about how to resolve his performance problem.

Sometimes, creating lasting change in a situation requires more than a mindfulness mindset and staying calm. When you notice that your thoughts or comments – or those of someone you work with – are particularly negative or stressful, it may be helpful to delve deeper into the mental realm. Remember how Mark's beliefs about his inability to manage down lowered his self-assurance as a leader. As a result, he didn't know what to do about Dana's crying. To develop a Confident leader mindset, he used the three Exploration Steps. First, he *listened* to his stressful thoughts like, "Things are falling apart." Then, he used The Work© to *inquire* about the impact of those negative thoughts. At the end of the inquiry process, he *affirmed* what was currently working well with Dana and his team. Then, he created a successful action plan that helped Dana overcome her crying and succeed with the payroll.

Once you're able to use Mindfulness and Exploration to develop calm and confidence, you're ready to develop a Powerful leader mindset by applying the Influence steps. Julie role-modeled how to courageously manage up. Despite her frustration with her boss' micromanaging, she used an effective strategy for influencing Renee's behavior. She initiated the conversation by *speaking* about a theoretical model – communications styles – that she knew was of interest to Renee. When Julie *observed* that Renee was enjoying the discussion about style types, she *focused* the conversation on her goal and asked permission to give feedback. As a result, Renee was open to negotiating Julie's request for more acknowledgement and autonomy.

I invite you to take The Mind to Lead challenge to train your mind for calm, confident, powerful leadership. Train your mind to notice when it's off course. Remember to be alert to the warning signals coming from your body, thoughts, feelings, and behavior. In general, have your **Reporter** be on the lookout for discomfort or stress. That's a pretty reliable sign that your mind has moved from "Now" to "Narrative."

When you notice that you have slipped into a stressful story about the past or the future, use your Executive Mind to return to the present moment. Look around and notice what's happening right now - including a few things that are working well. Take a mindful breath. If the situation is extremely challenging, explore the judgmental thoughts in your mind and the other person's mind. Be courageous and have the challenging conversation that you've been putting off. Try responding in new ways. Even a small step – a Pause before you respond – just might transform your professional relationship with another person forever.

And, remember, there's no one right way to do it. Just trust your instincts, and give it a try.

ACKNOWLEDGMENTS

Thank you to my clients for trusting me with your thoughts, hopes, fears, and dreams. It's an honor to support your work and to help you see that you're already the joyful, powerful leaders you wanted to become.

Thank you to the research teams of scientists like Jon Kabat-Zinn, Richard Davidson, and Dan Siegel whose work has made mindfulness more available to many people.

Thank you to my teachers and mentors, Pujari and Abhilasha, Shinzen Young, Eric Kolvig, Amy Schmidt, Shaila Tromovitch, Ajahn Amaro, Carol Wilson, Michelle McDonald, Ajahn Sumedho, and Rick Hanson.

Thank you to Byron Katie for creating The Work© and allowing me to share how I've used it with leaders.

Thank you to everyone who helped with the book. I appreciate early readings and feedback from Kim Russo, Robyn McCullough, and Brian Lesage. Thank you to my friend, Carolyn Stachowski, for the excellent anatomical structures she added on Mari Gayatari Stein's wonderful illustrations. Thank you to my brother, Jeff, for so much helpful feedback on the look and design of the book. Thank you to my exceptional editor, Carolyn Flynn, for holding a clear, big vision of the book and skillfully helping me create it. Thank you to my brilliant coach, Samantha Hartley, for helping me clarify how I help mindful leaders.

Thank you to my friends and family for your love and encouragement particularly my extraordinary healer, Dr. Sharon Esquibel, and my luminous friend, Britt Magadini, for shepherding me through patches of whitewater while writing the book and moving to Washington, D.C.

APPENDICES

APPENDIX I

FEELINGS LIST

MAD	SAD	GLAD	AFRAID
aggravated	agonizing	amused	anxious
appalled	depressed	appreciative	apprehensive
disgusted	dejected	delighted	cranky
dislike	despair	content	dread
displeased	despondent	eager	edgy
enraged	devastated	empowered	fidgety
furious	disappointed	encouraged	frazzled
frustrated	discouraged	enthusiastic	frightened
hate	disheartened	friendly	mistrustful
hostile	forlorn	glad	nervous
impatient	gloomy	happy	overwhelmed
irritated	grief	open	panicked
irked	heavy-hearted	pleased	petrified
incensed	hopeless	proud	scared
indignant	hurt	optimistic	stressed out
irate	lonely	safe	suspicious
livid	miserable	secure	terrified
outraged	unhappy	thankful	wary
resentful	upset	touched	worried

APPENDIX II

EARLY WARNING SIGNALS ASSESSMENT

The purpose of this assessment is to increase your awareness of stress-related symptoms in the absence of organic disease. I adapted it from several open source stress assessments I've used over the years.

Rate the frequency of each signal using this scale:

0   Never

1   Sometimes

2   Frequently

3   Almost always

Note: Any or all of these symptoms can be indicative of a medical condition. Any chronic symptoms should be referred to a medical professional.

Physical Signals

_____ 1. Headache

_____ 2. Eye Strain

_____ 3. Blushing

_____ 4. Teeth Grinding

_____ 5. Jaw clenching

_____ 6. Tight neck or shoulders

_____ 7. Rash

_____ 8. High Blood Pressure

_____ 9. Excessive sweating

_____ 10. Palpitations

_____ 11. Chest pain

_____ 12. Upset stomach

_____ 13. Shortness of breath

_____ 14. Constipation or diarrhea

_____ 15. Cold, clammy hands

_____ 16. Nervous tics

_____ 17. Curling toes

_____ 18. Back pain

_____ 19. Dizziness

Mental Signals

_____ 1. Forgetfulness

_____ 2. Excessive negative self-talk

_____ 3. Apathy

_____ 4. Fear of certain thoughts

_____ 5. Difficulty concentrating

_____ 6. Can't turn off certain thoughts or images

_____ 7. Loss of sexual interest or pleasure

_____ 8. Paranoia or feeling victimized

Emotional Signals

_____ 1. Depressed

_____ 2. Angry

_____ 3. Anxious

_____ 4. Irritable

_____ 5. Impatient

_____ 6. Feeling unsafe or very afraid

_____ 7. Lonely

_____ 8. Mistrustful

_____ 9. Unable or unwilling to forgive

_____ 10. Discouraged

_____ 11. Unresolved grief

_____ 12. Worried

Behavioral Signals

_____ 1. Increase or decrease in eating

_____ 2. Increase in smoking

_____ 3. Increase or decrease in sleep

_____ 4. Increase in drinking

_____ 5. Reckless driving

_____ 6. Compulsive gum chewing, whistling, or laughing

_____ 7. Increase in accidents or injuries

_____ 8. Unable to sit still

_____ 9. Increase or decrease in working

_____ 10. Unable to complete tasks

_____ 11. Increase in spending

_____ 12. Increase in gambling

_____ 13. Increase in entertainment: television, iPod, Internet, etc.

_____ 14. Excessive exercising

_____ 15. Excessive cleaning

_____ 16. Repetitive behaviors like checking, counting, or straightening that are meant to prevent or reduce anxiety

_____ 17. Bossiness or bullying

_____ 18. Withdrawal from relationships

Review your ratings on the four lists to identify the items with the highest scores. High scoring items are the ways that your body, mind, heart, and actor communicate that something is out of balance. Train your **Reporter** to _notice_ these signals as soon as they begin to surface.

Which of the signals on your checklists warrant a conversation with your health care provider? Contact a health care professional or organization to discuss any serious, repetitive, or long-term symptoms on the checklist.

APPENDIX III

MINDFULNESS PRACTICES

Most of the Mindfulness Practices (MPs) can be used either in a silent practice or during your workday, for example when you're in conversations or meetings. Before describing the MPs, here are tips for designing your silent practice, including the place and time, duration, posture, and style of practice.

PRACTICE PLACE AND TIME

Some people prefer to do their silent practice at work, because they want support for staying calm on the job. If you don't have a private office, find a quiet space at work that has a door like a conference room or supply room that you can reserve for practice time.

Some workplaces have a dedicated quiet space that anyone can use throughout the day for silent reflection. Even if people are coming and going in that room, it can be very supportive to silently practice mindfulness with others. Some worksites have mindfulness groups that practice together for 20 to 30 minutes every day. Ask your team if anyone wants to organize that type of regular session.

Select any time to practice at work as long as you can be relatively consistent. For example, you could practice as soon as you get to work, right before or after you eat lunch, or just before you leave for home.

If you prefer to do silent practice at home, again, select a consistent time and a quiet space. Some people like to practice as soon as they wake up or right before they go to bed. I don't practice mindfulness at night, because I find that it makes me too alert, and it's harder to fall asleep. Other people have the opposite experience. Some of my clients say that mindfulness practice clears their head at the end of a busy day. Try different times for your practice, and see what works best for you.

PRACTICE DURATION

Start with a goal of three to five minutes a day, three days a week. To keep track of the time, set a kitchen timer or watch alarm for your practice period rather than open-ing your eyes to check the clock. Three minutes might not sound like much, but it's better to win small, rather than lose big on a goal. After you've maintained a regular practice for a month or two, notice if you're eager to increase your practice time. When you're motivated to practice more, either increase the time by five-minute increments, or add one day a week. If you get up to 20-30 minutes of practice on four or five days a week, that's great.

Can a person do too much mindfulness practice? The average person probably won't hurt him or herself. However, if you have a history of mental illness or trauma, or if you're currently seeing a mental health professional, please discuss your mindfulness practice with a professional.

PRACTICE POSTURE

Here are some tips on how to use different body postures including sitting, stand-ing, lying down, and walking.

SEATED POSTURE

People often ask if they have to sit on the floor to do silent mindfulness practice. You might choose to sit on the floor if it's comfortable, though it's certainly not neces-sary. I recommend that most people, particularly those who are new to mindfulness practice, sit in a chair. Whichever surface you select, position your body so that it's erect though not rigid.

To practice on the floor, sit on a very thick cushion or bench so that your hips are higher than your knees. Sitting cushions are called zafus; benches are seizas. You can purchase either online. You can also sit on a stack of folded blankets. Whatever you select, place your seat at the front end of the surface, and cross your legs on the floor. Sitting with your hips slightly higher than your knees creates a slight arch in your low back and keeps your spine erect. This position is preferable to sitting flat on the floor with your knees up high and your head hunched forward.

When practicing in a chair, straight-backed is preferable to a recliner. You want to be comfortable, though not too cozy, or there's a tendency to fall asleep. While many of us could use more sleep, you want to strengthen your awareness during mindfulness rather than check out.

If your back is strong enough, sit on the front edge of the chair without your back resting against it. Place your ankles directly under your knees, so your knees are at a

90-degree angle.

Sitting away from the back of the chair requires some muscle strength. If you're unable to sit erect in this position for the entire period of mindfulness, that's fine. Whenever you need back support, scoot your hips back to the back of the chair first, and rest your spine lightly against the chair with knees still over ankles.

To position your head and neck, imagine you're a puppet, and someone is pulling up on a string attached to the top of your head. Your head gently lifts up, while your shoulders and chest relax downward. Some people bow their head forward while doing mindfulness practice. This isn't recommended, because it strains your neck and may induce sleepiness.

Place your hands in a comfortable position. You can lay each hand palm up or down on your legs, or cup them together with one palm on top of the other facing upward in your lap. Some people like to fold their arms across their chest. This can create tension in the chest or shoulders. However, if you feel more comfortable in this position, go for it.

OTHER POSTURES

You can practice most of the MPs while sitting, standing, or lying down. You can also practice a few while walking, though it's harder to do.

For standing practice, place your feet shoulder width apart, arms at your sides. Standing practice can be helpful when you're feeling jittery and don't want to sit still, or when you're sleepy. The effort it takes to hold your body in a standing position can sometimes reduce sleepiness. If you're sleepy, stand with your eyes open and gazing downward.

Practicing while lying down can be relaxing. However, avoid doing this when you're tired, or your practice might become a nap. My rule of thumb for lying practice is "mind alert, body hurt." When I have a headache or some other physical discomfort, lying down to practice helps my body relax. The relaxation sometimes helps me resist the pain less and explore it from a more neutral mindset.

Lie with your legs straight or bent at the knees. I prefer bent, because it feels better on my back and tells my body, "This isn't a nap; it's something different." If you notice you're getting drowsy, then sit up, stand up, or do some mindful walking.

YOUR EYES

During silent mindfulness practice, you can either close your eyes or keep them slightly open. If you keep your eyes open, gaze downward at the floor rather than look ahead or around the room. Even with the eyes closed, many people see images of colors, shapes, or objects. That's normal, so there's no need to get upset or try to make them stop. When you notice an image, simply return your awareness to your object of mindfulness.

PRACTICE STYLES

The two basic styles of mindfulness are Focused Awareness (FA) and Open Monitoring (OM) (Davidson and Lutz 2007, 176). In FA, you select an object of mindfulness, for example, your breath, and continuously return your awareness to it. In OM, you select a territory to scan, and *notice* what arises in it naturally.

The difference between the two styles is similar to what you can choose to notice at a baseball or basketball game. FA is like focusing your attention on one player regardless of what else is happening in the game. OM is like monitoring everything that's happening in the game. Instead of focusing on one player, your attention moves from one player to another, then to the strategy, fan reaction, the officials, or the giant TV screen. Your mind *notices* whatever is popping up into awareness in each successive moment. It's not that one way to watch a sporting event is better than another. The two styles just require different focusing muscles in your mind.

I recommend that beginners start with the FA technique, because it calms the mind, and teaches it to ignore distractions. After you've done FA regularly for several months, your mindfulness will be stronger, and you can try OM. OM lets your awareness move from one sensory experience to the next.

Over time, you'll be able to focus your awareness more easily. You won't have to try so hard to be mindful, because practicing MPs on a regular basis changes not only the function of your brain, but the structure.

This was shown by Sarah Lazar of Massachusetts General Hospital and her colleagues (Lazar et al. 2005, 1893). They did structural scans to compare the thickness of the brain in meditators and non-meditators. On average, the meditators had about nine years of meditation experience and practiced about six hours per week. Results showed that the regular practice of mindfulness meditation is associated with increased thickness in a set of cortical regions used during mindfulness practice. Those regions relate to hearing, seeing, and interoception – or, sensitivity to stimuli inside the body (Lazar et al. 2005, 1895).

The other interesting finding from this study is that regular mindfulness practice may slow age-related thinning – not of hair – but, of the frontal cortex at one spot. The average cortical thickness of the 40 to 50 year-old mindfulness practitioners was similar to the average thickness of the 20 to 30 year old practitioners and control subjects, suggesting that regular practice slows neural degeneration at that one spot (Lazar et al. 2005, 1896).

MINDFULNESS PRACTICES

The nine Mind to Lead MPs are organized according to the primary realm that they address: physical, mental, emotional, or behavioral (Table III.1). Select a mindfulness practice based on the type of stress you're experiencing or want to prevent. Most of these are physical practices that may reduce tension in the body; the other practices may help you address your thoughts, feelings, or actions.

TABLE III.1 THE MIND TO LEAD MINDFULNESS PRACTICES (MPs)

PHYSICAL MPs	Mindful breathing
	Body scan
	Sensation scan
	Feet and seat
	Mindful walking or wheeling
MENTAL MPs	Now or narrative
	Thinking about ...
EMOTIONAL MPs	Mindful feeling
BEHAVIORAL MPs	Right now I'm ...

PHYSICAL MPS

An effective way to quickly calm yourself is to simply be aware of your body as a whole or of a specific part. Shifting the mind's attention to body sensations takes the focus away from worrying. These five mindfulness practices increase awareness of sensations.

MINDFUL BREATHING

The breath is always available to help focus your mind and calm your body. While you can do this MP in any body position, I'll describe it in a seated position.

FIND YOUR NATURAL BREATH

To begin a practice period of Mindful Breathing, take a few breaths with the exhale longer than the inhale. Then, let go of control over the breath, and let it find its own natural rhythm. This concept is new for some people who believe the breath needs to be slow and deep in order for them to relax. Relaxation comes more from allowing what is happening than from prescribing a certain ideal state. The breath knows how it wants to be.

For example, when I'm nervous, my breath is short and shallow. Allowing my breath to be that way lets my body express, rather than repress, the fear by teaching myself, "It's okay to be scared. It's normal. I'm here to support you and will be patient until you feel safe again."

KINESTHETIC MINDFULNESS

After allowing the breath to find its own rhythm, *notice* what it feels like to *breathe*. Curiosity is a helpful attitude in mindfulness practice. Imagine that you've never had a breath before and are having this experience for the first time. What does it feel like?

As with all of the Physical MPs, Mindful Breathing is a kinesthetic practice. Kinesthesia is the perception or sensing of the motion, weight, or position of the body as muscles, tendons, and joints move. Rather than thinking about it or visualizing it, feel the breath as it moves into the nostrils, down the throat, fills the chest, and pushes the abdomen out. Then, feel the sensations as the breath moves out of the body.

At some point, probably within a few seconds, you'll notice that your awareness is distracted by other stimuli, usually a thought, body sensation, or sound. That's totally normal. No need to worry about that. Simply notice that the mind is distracted, and gently bring your awareness back to your breathing.

Notice the area in your body where you feel the breath most predominantly. You might feel the breath most in your abdomen, chest, nostrils, or some other place in your body. Pick one area, and place your awareness there. Feel your breath move in and out of that area.

After a few minutes, narrow your awareness in that area to a small spot. If you're focusing on your chest or abdomen, narrow your awareness to a spot about the size of a quarter. If you're focusing on your nose, select a spot about the size of a dime where your nostrils meet your upper lip.

As an option, you can add labeling. If you're focusing on an inhale in the abdomen or chest, say silently in the back of your mind, "rising." On the exhale, say "falling." If you're aware of the breath at the nostrils, you can note "in" on the inhale, and "out" on the exhale. If you're feeling the breath in some other part of your body, make up your own one-word labels to describe the movement of the breath.

Regardless of how often your awareness is distracted, bring it back to the breath. Mindfulness is more about the 'coming back' than the 'staying on.' The average mind isn't going to stay on the object of mindfulness with much consistency. Even an experienced practitioner's awareness will stray a lot, perhaps as much as a new practitioner's. The difference is that an experienced practitioner *notices* distractions sooner and doesn't get as upset. The game of mindfulness is noticing and coming back quickly and gently, rather than getting discouraged by self-judgments like, "I'm no good at mindfulness. My mind is out of control. I should give up."

FINE-TUNING AWARENESS OF SENSATIONS

If your awareness is relatively focused on the breath, you can choose to drop the labeling technique and focus on greater kinesthetic detail. Beyond the basic movement of the breath in and out, notice the qualities of sensation including:

- Pressure
- Temperature
- Vibration

Awareness of pressure means you sense the changing lightness or heaviness of the breath. Temperature means you sense the relative heat or cold at your breathing spot. Vibration means you perceive the pulse within your breathing spot. Sometimes vibration is too slow or subtle to discern. At other times, it'll be highly charged or jumpy. If you're unable to perceive vibration, don't worry about it. One way to differentiate between movement and vibration is to hold your breath for a moment and feel the pulsation without movement at the breathing spot. Don't hold your breath for long, because it's agitating.

BODY SCAN

Just as the breath is always with us, the body is here, too. Use your body as a kinesthetic gauge of how you're responding to what's happening now. You've probably had the experience of trusting your gut on something. That's what I mean by using your body as a gauge. Your body is like a giant compass that tells you which way to go, for example, whether to hire an employee or how to engage with a client or project.

The Body Scan MP connects you with your inner compass. You'll scan your whole body looking for clues and gathering information on which way to go. In mindfulness meditation, this technique is known as "sweeping," because you brush your awareness through your entire body. And, much like sweeping the floor, the scan sometimes has the perceived effect of moving debris out or cleaning up your internal space. Whether you experience this or not, the Body Scan allows the mind to label and acknowledge various sensations.

Before you begin, be aware of how much time you have to do the Body Scan. This will impact the speed at which you move awareness through your body. You can do a whole body scan in one or two seconds, or you can take thirty minutes. Obviously, the more time you take, the more information you get. However, you don't always have a large chunk of time. For example, you might want to do a quick body scan during a challenging meeting or when someone gives you surprising information.

SCANNING TOOL

Create a scanning tool to visually represent your awareness. For example, you can imagine your awareness as a laser beam or a cloth/sponge that "cleans" your inner landscape. The scanning tool should be something that you feel comfortable moving through your body. Someone told me he uses an image of a cheese grater. Ouch! That wouldn't work for me, however, if you like, use it.

Don't get hung up on creating a visually elaborate scanning tool. The goal of the Body Scan MP is to feel sensations in your body as opposed to seeing them. However, if you do see images of your body – either the surface or internal organs – as you scan through it, that's okay. Simply move the images to the background of your mind, and return your awareness to the sensations.

Your awareness or scanning tool will move as a thin horizontal plane from the top of the front of your body downwards. When it reaches the bottom or your feet, it will turn around and move up the back of your body. The scanning tool can change its size based on what it's moving through. For example, the tool is head-sized for your head, then finger-sized for your fingers. If you prefer to keep it one size that will cover every part of your body, that's fine, too.

BODY SCAN INSTRUCTIONS

Get in a comfortable, alert position. Either gaze downward or allow the eyes to gently close. See an image in your mind of your entire body as one unit. Place your awareness/scanning tool at the top of your head. See an image of your head as a three-dimensional object including your facial features, hair, and, if it feels comfortable, include your brain in the image. Move your scanning tool down through the front half of the three-dimensional space of your head as you notice any existing sensations. When your awareness encounters a sensation, spend only a moment acknowledging it. The acknowledgement might be recognizing the size, pressure, temperature, or vibration of the sensation.

You won't be able to catch all of that data on every sensation. Save that level of detailed scanning for the variation below called "Sensation Scan." Don't spend much time on any one sensation; keep the scanning tool moving downward. Remember compassionate awareness.

Give the tool a curious, neutral awareness as opposed to a judgmental charge. If your scanning tool could talk, I'd rather hear it say, "Gee, what an interesting pain. It makes sense that it's there right now," instead of, "Crap, I'm really tense. I'll never relax."

When your scanner gets through your head and neck, it'll be at the top of your chest. Move your scanning tool across one shoulder and down the front half of your arm into your hand and fingers. At the end of your fingers, turn around and go up the other side of the fingers and arm. Then, scan across your upper chest, and repeat on the other arm.

When you're back at the top of your chest, move down your torso into your pelvis. You're visually dividing your body in half vertically, and scanning only the front half. You'll scan the rear half of your body on the way up the backside.

When your scanner gets to the bottom of your torso, do the same thing with your legs that you did with your arms. Move your scanner down the front of one leg and into the feet and toes. At the end of the toes, turn around and go up the back half of the leg. Cross your pelvis, and go down the front and then up the back of the other leg.

Next, scan up the back half of your torso. When you reach your neck, scan up the back of your head to the top of your skull where you began. If you have more time, you can repeat the cycle. My website (www.themindtolead.com) has an audio file that's a ten-minute guided Body Scan.

VARIATION ON BODY SCAN: SENSATION SCAN

When you do a scan of your entire body, you might locate strong sensations with either a very pleasant or unpleasant charge. The purpose of the Sensation Scan is to investigate these strong sensations in more detail.

Since most people experience more stress than joy – particularly at work – most people have more unpleasant than pleasant sensations in the body. So, if you choose to try this, some of your Sensation Scans will be on sensations that are painful or prickly. That's okay. I want you to get used to, and even accepting of, unpleasant sensations.

And, I strongly encourage you to do Sensation Scans on pleasant sensations. When something great happens at work, stop for at least 30 seconds to fully experience it in your body. When you submit a proposal before the deadline, where do you experience delight? When an employee grievance against you is dismissed, how do you sense relief in your body? When a super star leaves her company to work with you, what does excitement feel like?

Take time to feel success and happiness in your body. *Notice* more frequently that you already have the life you always wanted. You're a success right now! Even if you just graduated from college, were recently promoted to first-line supervisor, or haven't gotten a raise in two years. At least you got to where you are right now by taking small steps toward your ultimate goal. *Notice* how great that success feels in your body. Enjoy the small steps today, so that you can more fully feel the big wins in the future.

SENSATION SCAN INSTRUCTIONS

To begin the Sensation Scan, select a strong sensation in your body. It can be either pleasant or unpleasant. You can examine a sensation that you discovered during a Body Scan, or you can use one that surfaces during the day.

Get into a comfortable, erect position while sitting, standing, or lying down. *Allow* the strong sensation to pull your awareness into it. Get a general sense of the sensation. In your mind, draw a line around the sensation, so that you have an idea of where it begins and ends in your body. Don't worry about being precise. The edges of the sensation may extend further into the body than you were originally aware of; some edges might feel fuzzy or vague. That's normal. Just get a picture of how much space, in general, the sensation occupies in your body. Is it the size of a dime, grapefruit, or basketball? If you like, give the sensation a color.

Pick one edge or side of the sensation, and place your scanning tool there. Move your awareness/scanning tool through the sensation from one side to the other. If it's a small sensation, for example, the size of a quarter, move your scanning tool through it in a uni-directional manner. For example, if you placed your awareness at the top or bottom of the sensation, scan vertically toward the other edge. If you started on the left or right side of the sensation, scan horizontally to the other side.

If you're focusing on a large sensation, scan it in a bi-directional manner in order to pick up information from the entire sensation. By bi-directional, I mean your scanning tool will simultaneously move vertically and horizontally.

Uni-directional versus bi-directional scanning is like the difference between washing a small saucer versus a large platter. When you hold a saucer in one hand, the other hand can wipe across the entire face of it in one pass. You might pass back and forth across the saucer, but a sponge in your hand is large enough to clean the whole saucer by moving in that one plane. Similarly, use unidirectional scanning for small sensations.

A platter, however, is much bigger than your hand. To wash a large platter, you hold it in one hand and place your sponge at one edge. As you move the sponge up and down in the vertical plane of the platter, you simultaneously scrub across the horizontal plane of the platter, so that you clean the entire surface. Use this bi-directional style for scanning large sensations. Begin at one edge of the sensation, and move your awareness up and down while you simultaneously move horizontally to the other side.

Remember that your Body Scan was three-dimensional. You didn't just scan the surface of your face. You passed your scanning tool through everything behind your face including your eyeballs, sinuses, and teeth. Make your Sensation Scan three-dimensional, too.

What are you looking for? Whatever's there. Simply scan your awareness back and forth at a relatively slow pace. Your awareness is like a Mars rover moving across a topography that changes from flat, barren land to rolling hills and then to jagged peaks. Throughout your journey, collect information about the sensation's three physical qualities: pressure, temperature, and vibration. Your scanning tool is neutral, not judging. It simply witnesses what's there.

Your awareness might *notice* a piece of the sensation that has a greater density or stronger qualities than the rest of it. That area is called the "hot spot," even though it could be extremely cold. It has a more intense pressure, stronger temperature, or different vibration. If you encounter a hot spot, stop there for a few moments. Crawl down into it with your scanning tool, and just hang out. There's no need to be afraid. It's just a strong sensation, like a bolt of lightning or crack of thunder. It won't kill you. *Notice*, *breathe*, and *allow* it. Be curious and accepting.

You don't have to find words to describe the hot spot or try to figure out what it means. Simply communicate with the hot spot by "listening" to its pressure, temperature, and vibration. You can stay in the hot spot as long as you like, or you can return to scanning the whole sensation. Staying in the hot spot is like sitting in a hot tub, (okay, it's probably not that pleasant); simply feel the jets, warmth, and bubbles without having to describe them.

How long should you scan a sensation? If you *notice* a strong sensation during a challenging conversation, you might only have a few seconds to scan it during the meeting. If the sensation is still bothering you later that day, take five to ten minutes or more to gently scan back and forth through it. The goal is to acknowledge it, rather than try to make it go away.

As you finish your practice period, *notice* if anything changed in the sensation. Is it the same size, density, and temperature? *Notice* if anything changed in your thoughts or emotional state.

FEET & SEAT

Feet & Seat is one of the most popular MPs that I teach to leaders. They like it, because it's easy to do and instantly relaxing.

FEET & SEAT INSTRUCTIONS

Sit in a chair with both feet flat on the floor and your ankles underneath your knees. Notice that you have two feet resting on the floor. Lift your toes up slightly and wiggle them for a few seconds. Relax your toes. Focus on one foot. Move your scanning tool through the bottom of the foot for a few seconds while sensing the pressure, temperature, and vibration. Repeat the scan on your other foot. Notice how one foot feels different from the other. Focus your awareness on both feet simultaneously. You don't have to catch every sensation. Just keep a general sense of your feet in your awareness. Take a breath in. As you exhale, let your feet be heavy and sink into the floor.

Next, notice that you're sitting in a chair. Move the awareness into the back of your legs where they contact the chair. Move your scanning tool up the back of your legs, across your seat, and up to the point where your back no longer contacts the chair. Sense the pressure, temperature, and vibration in the back side of your body, your seat. You don't have to catch every sensation. Just keep a general sense of your seat in your awareness. Take a breath in. As you exhale, let your seat be heavy and sink into the chair.

If possible, hold an awareness of your feet and seat simultaneously. You don't need to scan, just hold a sense of the pressure of feet on the floor and seat in the chair. If you prefer, you can hold an awareness of just one, either your feet or your seat. Take a breath in. As you exhale, let your feet and seat be heavy and sink down.

RESEARCH ON THE FEET MP

Another reason I like this MP is that a research study confirmed the effectiveness of feeling your feet. In their study, Singh and colleagues selected three people who were frequently readmitted to a psychiatric hospital because of anger management problems (Singh et al. 2007). They taught the individuals to shift their attention and awareness from any anger-producing situation to the soles of their feet, which is a neutral point on the body. After learning the feet mindfulness technique, the three individuals showed no physical aggression and very low rates of verbal aggression over four years of follow-up.

MINDFUL WALKING

When you alternate periods of sitting and walking practice, it can balance the mind and body. In sitting practices, you close the eyes and focus awareness on the motionless body. It's a very still, internal practice. In mindful walking, your body moves through space and time. It's an energizing practice where you interact with the environment.

I recommend that you do some sitting and some walking as part of your weekly mindfulness practice. For example, if you built up to doing a sitting practice for 20 minutes, four days a week, you could divide that up by sitting one day, and then walking the next day. Or, you could divide your practice time, so that you do ten minutes of walking followed by ten minutes of sitting. Experiment with different options, and notice the effects of the different combinations. There's no one right way to design your practice; simply notice what feels most supportive to you.

MINDFUL WALKING INSTRUCTIONS

There are two kinds of walking practice: formal and informal. Formal practice is done in silence for an uninterrupted period of time, from five to 60 minutes. It's done with the eyes gazing downward and the legs moving very slowly. Once you learn how to do formal walking practice, you can do informal brief periods of mindful walking throughout your day.

In informal practice, for example, you can walk mindfully from the parking lot or mass transit stop to your office. You can feel your feet contact the floor as you walk down the hall to use the copy machine or meet with a colleague. There's no need to go slowly, gaze downward, or be silent. Use your normal gait, look around and talk with people. Simply keep a large percentage of your awareness on the sensations in your feet.

For formal walking practice, select an environment that is relatively quiet where you won't be interrupted. You'll need about ten feet of open space for your walking lane. If you don't have adequate space in your office, find a conference room or unused hallway. Some people do their walking practice on an empty stairwell. If your knees can handle slow stepping up and down for ten minutes or so, go for it. You'll train your mind, and build firm buns!

Once you've selected your walking space, stand in an erect, relaxed posture with the top of your head gently pulling up and your arms relaxed at your sides. Without bending your head forward too much, gaze downward so that you're looking at the floor about three to four feet in front of you. Feel your feet in contact with the floor. Begin by walking in a slower than normal pace. When you reach the end of your walking lane, stop and mindfully turn around. Continue walking back and forth on the path while focusing on the sensations in your feet.

If you like, add labeling to help focus your awareness. Use the labels "left, right" to track when your left foot contacts the floor, then your right.

If your walking pace naturally slows down, begin to label finer gradations of movement such as the "lifting, moving, placing" of each foot. Say each label softly in your mind just once. "Lifting" describes the foot's takeoff and movement up. "Moving" expresses when the foot travels forward through space. "Placing" begins as the foot begins its descent, and ends when it contacts the floor. Keep your body movement fluid and the labeling very soft in the back of your mind. Most of your awareness will be on the sensations in the feet.

Mindful walking can become very enjoyable. You might notice a deep appreciation for how parts of your body work well together and how amazing it is that you can move yourself from place to place.

Before the appreciation, though, there could be frustration. It's common for beginners to lose your balance, because you're not used to slow movement. The solution is to either slow down a bit more, so that you can control your movement, or speed up so that your pace is closer to normal walking.

MINDFUL WHEELING

For leaders in a wheelchair, follow the preparatory steps for mindful walking by selecting a quiet environment with at least ten feet for a wheeling lane. Sit with your hands in your lap. Based on your ability to feel sensations, notice the feel of your hands in your lap or where your body contacts the chair. Inhale, and as you exhale, let your body relax into the chair.

If you're able to move your arms, slowly move one or both hands with awareness to grasp the wheel(s) of your chair. If you normally drive with one hand, leave the other hand relaxed in your lap. Feel your hand contacting the wheel. With awareness, turn the wheel forward slowly until you reach the bottom of the arc. Release your hand, and slowly move it back to the top of the wheel. Adjust the amount of tension in your hand, so that you can grasp the wheel firmly without clenching it. Use the labels "grasp, push, move" to describe grabbing the wheel, pushing it forward to the bottom of the arc, and moving your hand through space back to the top of the wheel. Or, create your own labels that describe the basic movements of slow wheeling.

When you reach the end of your wheeling path, slowly turn your chair around, and continue mindful wheeling back to your starting point. Just as a mindful leader who walks will focus primarily on sensations in her feet but may notice her legs, place your awareness mostly on sensations in your hands, but also be sensitive to your arms.

Thanks to an online article by Matthew Huston that inspired me to create this MP (www.themindfulnessbell.org).

MENTAL MPS

Much of our stress begins with negative thinking. The purposes of the Mental MPs are to help you notice when stressful thinking occurs and help you cope with it.

NOW OR NARRATIVE

You can use this MP during silent practice or while you're doing routine tasks like getting dressed, cooking, or putting paper in the copy machine. While you sit silently or do a task, notice if your awareness is either in the present moment or in a narrative. The narrative, or story, will be about the past or future.

When your awareness is in the present moment, you'll notice your current experience through one of your senses – seeing, hearing, touching, tasting, or smelling. When you experience something in the present moment, gently label in the back of your mind, "Now." For example, as you *notice* the feeling of reaching for and touching a stack of paper, label, "Now." As you notice the taste of a sip of coffee, label, "Now." As you notice that you're looking around the conference room and seeing different colleagues, label, "Now."

On the other hand, when you notice that your mind is in a narrative about the past or the future, gently label in the back of your mind, "Narrative." Don't try to edit or stop your thoughts. Simply notice that your mind is telling a story, almost as if you would *notice* that someone else is talking. After you *notice* that your mind is in a narrative, your awareness might come back to the present moment and *notice* what's happening right now. If that happens, notice what you are experiencing through your senses, and gently label, "Now."

THINKING ABOUT

I hope the title of this MP isn't confusing. This practice isn't prescriptive; you're not going to tell yourself to think about something. Instead, it's a descriptive practice. You'll simply watch the content of your thoughts, and describe it with labels. When you become aware via your **Reporter** that you're upset or even happy about something, use this practice to get a print out of the thoughts. Thinking About is particularly helpful when you have a repetitive thought – either pleasant or unpleasant – that just won't go away.

INSTRUCTIONS FOR THINKING ABOUT

Label the general topic of your thoughts silently to yourself or aloud by saying, "Thinking about _____" (fill in the blank with a short topic rather than the entire thought). Continue to repeat the labeling process every three to five seconds. *Notice* if the topic changes or stays the same.

Let's say, for example, that while you're walking to a meeting, you notice that you're really dreading it. Your **Reporter** picks up a queasy, rumbling sensation in your stomach that extends into your chest as a pressure or constriction. You notice that you're barely breathing, so you take a deep inhalation and wonder what thoughts are connected to this pain.

You tune into your **Reporter's** account of the situation. As you hear your thoughts, you're able to label what you're thinking about: "Thinking about Joe…Thinking about Joe bugs me…Thinking about meetings are boring…Thinking about lack of decisions…Thinking about work overload."

Sometimes, simply being a bit more aware of your thoughts will calm or slow the thinking process. However, don't try to make your thoughts go away. Be gentle.

Observe that thinking is happening. The Thinking About practice also gives you the opportunity to *notice* how your thoughts impact your behavior.

EMOTIONAL MP

Practicing the Physical and Mental MPs can give you a solid foundation in awareness of sensations and thoughts, the two ingredients of a feeling. The purpose of doing the Emotional MP – Mindful Feeling – is to receive feeling information from yourself to improve your intrapersonal attunement and hopefully be more ready to attune with others.

MINDFUL FEELING

When a person tells me that she can't identify her feelings, I might suggest that she begin by doing Physical or Mental MPs. Once a person gets comfortable writing her thoughts and noticing body sensations, she can usually identify her basic feelings. If you have a similar challenge, begin by asking yourself if you generally feel good or bad. Narrow that sense to one of the four emotion categories: mad, sad, glad, or afraid. Review the Feelings List (Appendix I) to select an emotion that feels close enough to what you're experiencing. Those steps will help you do the Mindful Feeling practice.

INSTRUCTIONS FOR MINDFUL FEELING

When you're experiencing strong emotions, for example, you're upset, confused, or happy, take from 30 seconds to ten minutes to name your feelings. Just as you named your thoughts in the Thinking About MP, label your emotions – about every three to five seconds – silently in your mind or say them out loud like, "Fear," "Anger," "Sadness."

Observe your feelings without trying to make them stop or without acting on them inappropriately. Be gentle. Simply observe and label your feelings as they happen.

If you find this MP beneficial, try it for a longer period of time, like 20 minutes. It can be an interesting way to get to know yourself. You might *notice* your emotions changing over the course of 20 minutes, for example, "Anxious" turns to "Concerned" then to "Curious."

BEHAVIORAL MP

The Behavioral MP helps you notice your actions. Collecting and analyzing information about your behavior helps you create lasting change in yourself and others.

RIGHT NOW I'M...

This MP is similar to the Thinking About practice, except that you'll note what you're doing rather than what you're thinking. Right Now I'm... helps you stay in the present moment during longer tasks like clearing a paper jam from the copy machine or packing your suitcase before a trip.

To do this practice, state what is currently happening – either silently in your mind or aloud – by completing the phrase, "Right now I'm _____." For example, label your arrival at work, "Right now, I'm driving into the parking lot. Now, I'm walking into the building. Now, I'm waiting for the elevator. Now, I'm saying hello to people. Now, I'm hanging up my coat. Now, I'm checking my to-do list." About every ten seconds or so, label what is currently happening.

You don't have to label like this all day! Do it when you notice that a narrative about the past or future distracts your mind. Bringing your attention into the present moment helps you worry less, as well as increase your effectiveness and contentment with what's happening now.

INFLUENCE TOOLS

INFLUENCE STEPS

SPEAK – OBSERVE – FOCUS

1. *Speak* your expectation in a concise statement to the other person.

2. *Observe* the other person's reaction.

3. *Focus* the other person's mind on your expected outcome.

INFLUENCE TOOLS

LASER MESSAGE: Twelve words or less that communicate your expectation

PAUSE: Silence

VENTING: Complaining for up to five minutes

FACTS & FEELINGS: You feel _____ (feeling) about _____ (fact).

OPEN-ENDED QUESTIONS: Who, What, When, Where, How

BEER:

1. Behavior   When you _____

2. Effect   The impact on (clients, the team, you, etc.) is _____

3. Emotion   I feel _____

4. Request/Require I request/require that you _____

FLEXING TO FOUR STYLES

1. Leading   task-oriented extrovert

• Acknowledge the Leader's leadership strengths.

• Ask "Who" questions that point out the impact on others: "Who will be satisfied with this option?"

2. Socializing   people-oriented extrovert

• Acknowledge the Socializer's contributions with fun, authentic praise.

• Ask "When" questions to get a commitment on a specific deadline: "You've got a lot on your plate. When are you absolutely positive you can deliver this spread sheet?"

3. Thinking   task-oriented introvert

- Acknowledge that the Thinker is doing what you expected.
- Ask "What" questions to elicit concerns and ideas: "What could we do to improve customer service response time?"

4. Relating   people-oriented introvert

- Acknowledge that the Relater is loyal and dependable.
- Ask "How" questions to elicit ideas on how procedures and systems could be improved: "How can I do a better job updating you on my team's progress?"

APPENDIX V

RESOURCES

HOW TO FIND A COACH

The International Coaching Foundation has an excellent search engine for finding a coach for your work or personal life: www.coachfederation.com

For articles on leadership coaching, how to find a coach, and what to look for when interviewing potential coaches: www.theMindtoLead.com

HOW TO FIND A COUNSELOR

The National Board for Certified Counselors allows you to search by specialty and location: www.nbcc.org

SUGGESTED READING

BRAIN AND MIND

Hanson, Rick and Richard Mendius. *Buddha's Brain: The Practical Neuroscience of Happiness, Love and Wisdom.* Oakland: New Harbinger, 2009.

Medina, John. *Brain Rules: 12 Principles for Surviving and Thriving at Work, Home and School.* Seattle: Pear Press, 2008.

Siegel, Dan. *The Mindful Brain: Reflection and Attunement in the Cultivation of Well-Being.* New York: W.W. Norton & Company, Inc., 2007.

COMMUNICATION

Rosenberg, Marshall B. *Nonviolent Communication: A Language of Life*, Puddledancer Press, 2003, 2nd edition.

MINDFULNESS

Goldstein, Joseph. *The Experience of Insight: A Simple and Direct Guide to Buddhist Meditation.* Boston: Shambala, 1987.

Kabat-Zinn, Jon. *Full Catastrophe Living: Using the Wisdom of Your Body and Mind to Face*

Stress, Pain, and Illness. Delta, 1990.

Salzberg, Sharon. *Lovingkindness: The Revolutionary Art of Happiness.* Boston: Shambala, 1995.

Wright, Laura. *Quiet Mind, Open Heart: Finding Inner Peace through Reflection, Journaling, and Meditation.* Bristlecone Publishing, 2008.

THE WORK ©

www.thework.com

Byron Katie. Instructions for Doing The Work. 2011. http://www.thework.com/downloads/instructions_for_thework.pdf.

Byron Katie. Judge Your Neighbor Worksheet. 2011. http://www.thework.com/downloads/JudgeYourNeighbor.pdf.

Byron Katie and Michael Katz. *I Need Your Love - Is That True?: How to Stop Seeking Love, Approval, and Appreciation and Start Finding Them Instead.* New York: Three Rivers Press, 2006.

Byron Katie and Stephen Mitchell. *Loving What Is: Four Questions That Can Change Your Life.* New York: Three Rivers Press, 2003.

Byron Katie and Stephen Mitchell. *A Thousand Names for Joy: Living in Harmony with the Way Things Are.* New York: Three Rivers Press, 2008.

TIME MANAGEMENT

Allen, David. *Getting Things Done: The Art of Stress-Free Productivity.* New York: Penguin Group, 2001.

MINDFULNESS RETREAT CENTERS IN THE USA

Do an Internet search on "Mindfulness Retreat + (your city or state)." The largest US centers are:

Spirit Rock Meditation Center, Woodacre, CA. www.spiritrock.org

Insight Meditation Society, Barre, MA. www.dharma.org

APPENDIX VI

GLOSSARY

ATTUNEMENT Receiving, interpreting, and reflecting back to a person the signals you pick up about the four realms of his/her experience. In interpersonal attunement, the person is someone else. In intrapersonal attunement, the person is you.

BEER A four-step formula for communicating feedback by describing a Behavior, Effect, Emotion, and Request.

BOTTOM-UP PROCESSING When sensory information comes into the body, up the brain stem, enters the bottom of the neocortex, and moves up to the processing centers.

BRAIN One-pound organ in skull from which thought, emotion, and control of body activities emanates.

BROKEN RECORD A Laser statement repeated as often as necessary to *focus* the other person's mind on the issue.

FACTS & FEELINGS An attunement tool to reflect back the event and emotion that you think another person is experiencing.

FOCUSED AWARENESS One of two styles of mindfulness practice in which you continually return your awareness to a specific object of mindfulness, for example, your breath. The other style of mindfulness is Open Monitoring.

FOUR REALMS Domains through which people experience life including physical (body sensations), mental (thoughts, memories, ideas), emotional (feelings), and behavioral (actions, nonverbal and verbal communication).

LABELING Mindfulness tool of saying one or two words to describe what you are experiencing; labeling is done by the **Reporter** either aloud or silently in the back of the mind.

LASER MESSAGE A statement that is delivered in 12 words or less to focus the conversation on your intention or goal.

MIND Defined by Dan Siegel as the "process that regulates the flow of energy and information" (Siegel 2007, 5).

MINDFUL LEADER   A person responsible for guiding one or more people toward a common goal who uses a leadership style called Calm, Confident Power that develops as a result of applying Mindfulness, Exploration, and Influence tools to more effectively notice and motivate oneself and others for lasting change.

MINDFULNESS   Defined by Jon Kabat-Zinn as "the awareness that emerges through paying attention on purpose, in the present moment, and nonjudgmentally to the unfolding of experience moment by moment" (Kabat-Zinn 2003, 145-146). Also known as mindful awareness. See the two types of mindfulness practice: Focused Awareness and Open Monitoring.

MINDSETS   The three states of mind that leaders want most: Calm developed through Mindfulness, Confident developed through Exploration, and Power developed through Influence.

NEOMAMMALIAN BRAIN/NEOCORTEX   Outermost layer of the brain and home of executive functions including language, logic, visuospatial, intuitive processes, and motor control of body.

NEUROLEADERSHIP   Term created by David Rock and Jeffery Schwartz in 2006 to describe an innovative field that blends leadership development with an understanding of how the mind works.

NEUROPLASTICITY   The brain's ability to reorganize itself by forming new neural connections that lead to functional improvements in emotional balance, immune function, and stress response.

NOTICE   Being aware of what's happening in the present moment in oneself or others in one or more of the four realms of experience – physical, mental, emotional, and behavioral.

OBJECT OF MINDFULNESS   What you intend to focus on – the realm, sense, or specific experience like breathing – during a period of mindfulness.

OPEN MONITORING   One of two styles of mindfulness practice in which you select a realm, sense, or physical territory to scan, and notice what occurs in it naturally. The other style of mindfulness practice is Focused Awareness.

PALEOMAMMALIAN BRAIN   Located in the limbic system, it's the seat of emotion.

PROJECTION   Crediting others with your own unacknowledged desires or traits.

REACTIVITY   Responding without noticing what's happening or without consciously choosing appropriate steps to take.

REPORTER   The calm, unbiased, curious quality of the mind that observes and reports (labels) your experience without overreacting.

REPTILIAN BRAIN   Located in the cerebellum and brain stem, it's the oldest layer of the brain and controls breathing, heartbeat, and establishing territory.

SOCIAL INTELLIGENCE   The ability to identify and impact the feelings and behavior of yourself and of others.

TOP-DOWN PROCESSING   When upper levels of the neocortex send ideas and past information down to lower levels in response to stimuli.

TRIUNE BRAIN   The three layers of the brain that evolved over millions of years: Reptilian (cerebellum and brain stem), Paleomammalian (limbic system), and Neomammalian (neocortex).

THE WORK©   A simple yet powerful inquiry process developed by Byron Katie that teaches how to identify and question thoughts that cause stress (Byron Katie 2003, 2006, 2008).

REFERENCES

Allen, David. *Getting Things Done: The Art of Stress-Free Productivity.* New York: Penguin Group, 2001.

Baer, Ruth A., Gregory T. Smith, Jaclyn Hopkins, Jennifer Krietemeyer, and Leslie Toney. "Using self-report assessment methods to explore facets of mindfulness." Assessment 13, no. 1, 27-45, 2006.

Butler, Emily A., Boris Egloff, Frank H. Wilhelm, Nancy C. Smith, Elizabeth A. Erickson, and James J. Gross. "The social consequences of expressive suppression." Emotion 3, no. 1, 48-67, 2003.

Byron Katie. "Instructions for Doing The Work," 2011 http://www.thework.com/downloads/instructions_for_thework.pdf.

Byron Katie. "Judge Your Neighbor Worksheet," 2011. http://www.thework.com/downloads/JudgeYourNeighbor.pdf.

Byron Katie and Michael Katz. *I Need Your Love - Is That True?: How to Stop Seeking Love, Approval, and Appreciation and Start Finding them Instead.* New York: Three Rivers Press, 2006.

Byron Katie and Stephen Mitchell. *Loving What Is: Four Questions That Can Change Your Life.* New York: Three Rivers Press, 2003.

Byron Katie and Stephen Mitchell. *A Thousand Names for Joy: Living in Harmony with the Way Things Are.* New York: Three Rivers Press, 2008.

Crawley, Jim and Jan Grant. "Emotionally focused therapy for couples and attachment theory." *Australian & New Zealand Journal of Family Therapy* 26, no. 2, 82-89, 2005.

Creswell, J. David, Baldwin M. Way, Naomi I. Eisenberger, and Matthew D. Lieberman. "Neural correlates of dispositional mindfulness during affect labeling," *Psychosomatic Medicine* 69, 560-565, 2007.

Davidson, Richard J., Jon Kabat-Zinn, Jessica Schumacher, Melissa Rosenkrantz, Daniel Muller, Saki F. Santorelli, Ferris Urbanowski, Anne Harrington, Katherine Bonus, and John F. Sheridan. 2003. "Alterations in brain and immune function produced by mindfulness meditation," *Psychosomatic Medicine* 65, no. 4, 564-570.

Davidson, Richard J. and Antoine Lutz. "Buddha's Brain: Neuroplasticity and meditation," *IEEE Signal Processing Magazine*, 176, 172-174, January 2007.

Eisenberger, Naomi I., Johanna M. Jarcho, Matthew D. Lieberman, and Bruce D. Naliboff. "An experimental study of shared sensitivity to physical and social rejection," *Pain* 126, 132-138, 2006.

Ekman, Paul. *Emotions Revealed: Recognizing Faces and Feelings to Improve Communication and Emotional Life.* New York: Holt Paperbacks, 2007.

Ekman, Paul, Richard J. Davidson, Matthieu Ricard, and B. Alan Wallace. "Buddhist and psychological perspectives on emotions and well-being," *Current Directions in Psychological Science* 14, no. 2, 59-63, 2005.

Gardner, Howard. *Frames of Mind: The Theory of Multiple Intelligences.* New York: Basic Books, 1983.

Gardner, Howard. *Changing Minds: The Art and Science of Changing Our Own and Other People's Minds.* Boston: Harvard Business School Press, 2004.

Goldapple, Kimberly, Zindel Segal, Carol Garson, Mark Lau, Peter Bieling, Sidney Kennedy, and Helen Mayberg. "Modulation of cortical-limbic pathways in major depression: treatment-specific effects of Cognitive Behavior Therapy." *Archives of General Psychiatry* 61, 34-41, 2004.

Goleman, Daniel. *Working with Emotional Intelligence.* New York: Bantam Books, 1998.

Goleman, Daniel. *Social Intelligence: The New Science of Human Relationships.* New York: Bantam Books, 2007.

Gottman, J. *Why Marriages Succeed or Fail: And How You Can Make Yours Last.* New York: Simon and Schuster, 1995.

Hanson, Rick and Richard Mendius. *Buddha's Brain: The Practical Neuroscience of Happiness, Love, and Wisdom.* Oakland: New Harbinger, 2009.

Hersey, Paul, Ken Blanchard, and Dewey E. Johnson. "Management of organizational behavior: Leading human resources." 8th edition. New York: Prentice Hall, 2000.

Huston, Matthew. *The Turning of My Wheels,* www.themindfulnessbell.org.

Iacoboni, Marco. *Mirroring People: The New Science of How We Connect with Others.* New York: Farrar, Straus & Giroux, New York, 2008.

Kabat-Zinn, Jon. "Mindfulness-based interventions in context: Past, present, and future." *Clinical Psychology: Science and Practice* 10, no. 2, 144-156, 2003.

Keppe, Norberto. *The Origin of Illness: Psychological, Physical and Social.* Englewood Cliffs: Campbell Hall Press, 2002.

Lazar, Sara W., Catherine E. Kerr, Rachel H. Wasserman, Jeremy R. Gray, Douglas N. Greve, Michael T. Treadway, Metta McGarvey, Brian T. Quinn, Jeffrey A. Dusek, Herbert Benson, Scott L. Rauch, Christopher I. Moore, and Bruce Fischl. "Meditation experience is associated with increased cortical thickness," *NeuroReport* 16, no. 17, 1893-1897, 2005.

Lieberman, Matthew D., Naomi I. Eisenberger, Molly J. Crockett, Sabrina M. Tom, Jennifer H. Pfeifer, and Baldwin M. Way. "Putting feelings into words: Affect labeling disrupts amygdala activity in response to affective stimuli." *Psychological Science* 18, no. 5, 421-428, 2007.

Lutz, Antoine, Lawrence L. Greischar, Nancy B. Rawlings, Matthieu Ricard, and Richard J. Davidson. 2004. "Long-term meditators self-induce high-amplitude gamma synchrony during mental practice," proceedings of the National Academy of Sciences 101, no. 46, 16369-16373.

Lutz, Antoine, Julie Brefczynski-Lewis, Tom Johnstone, and Richard J. Davidson. "Regulation of the neural circuitry of emotion by compassion meditation: Effects of meditative expertise." PLoS ONE 3, no. 3, 1-10: e1897. doi:10.1371/journal.pone.0001897, 2008.

MacLean, Paul. *The Triune Brain in Evolution: Role in Paleocerebral Functions.* New York: Springer, 1990.

Medina, John. *Brain Rules: 12 Principles for Surviving and Thriving at Work, Home and School.* Seattle: Pear Press, 2008.

Raichle, M.E., A. M. MacLeod, A. Z. Snyder, W. J. Powers, D. A. Gusnard, and G. L. Shumlan. "A default mode of brain function," proceedings of the National Academy of Sciences, 98: 676-682, 2001.

Rock, David. *Your Brain at Work: Strategies for Overcoming Distraction, Regaining Focus, and Working Smarter All Day Long.* New York: HarperCollins, 2009.

Rock, David and Jeffrey Schwartz. "The neuroscience of leadership." *strategy+business* 4, 1-10, 2006.

Rosenberg, Marshall B. *Nonviolent Communication: A Language of Life.* Encinitas: Puddledancer Press, 2003, 2nd edition.

Salzberg, Sharon. *Lovingkindness: The Revolutionary Art of Happiness.* Boston: Shambala, 1995.

Schwartz, Jeffrey M. *Brain Lock: Free Yourself from Obsessive-Compulsive Behavior.* New York: HarperCollins, 1996.

Siegel, Daniel J. *Mindsight: The New Science of Personal Transformation.* New York: Bantam Books, 2010.

Siegel, Daniel J. *The Mindful Brain: Reflection and Attunement in the Cultivation of Well-Being.* New York: W.W. Norton & Company, Inc., 2007.

Siegel, Daniel J. "Toward an interpersonal neurobiology of the developing mind: Attachment relationships, "mindsight," and neural integration." *Infant Mental Health Journal* 22, no. 1-2, 67-94, 2001.

Singh, Nirbhay N., Giulio E. Lancioni, Alan S. W. Winton, Angela D. Adkins, Robert G. Wahler, Mohamed Sabaawi, and Judy Singh. "Individuals with mental illness can control their aggressive behavior through mindfulness training," *Behavior Modification* 31, no. 3, 313-328, 2007.

INDEX

ABOUT THE AUTHOR

Suzanne Kryder, Ph.D., owns a Washington, D.C.-based neuroleadership training and coaching company that blends leadership development with an understanding of how the mind works. Her brain-based coaching model, The Mind to Lead, combines 25+ year backgrounds in management development and mindfulness meditation. She has trained and coached thousands of leaders in the public and private sectors to be more effective. She has practiced mindfulness meditation since 1985 and has a training certification from Spirit Rock Meditation Center in Woodacre, Calif., to teach classes and daylong retreats. Suzanne is a co-founder and host of the award-winning public radio series, Peace Talks Radio. Find her at TheMindtoLead.com.